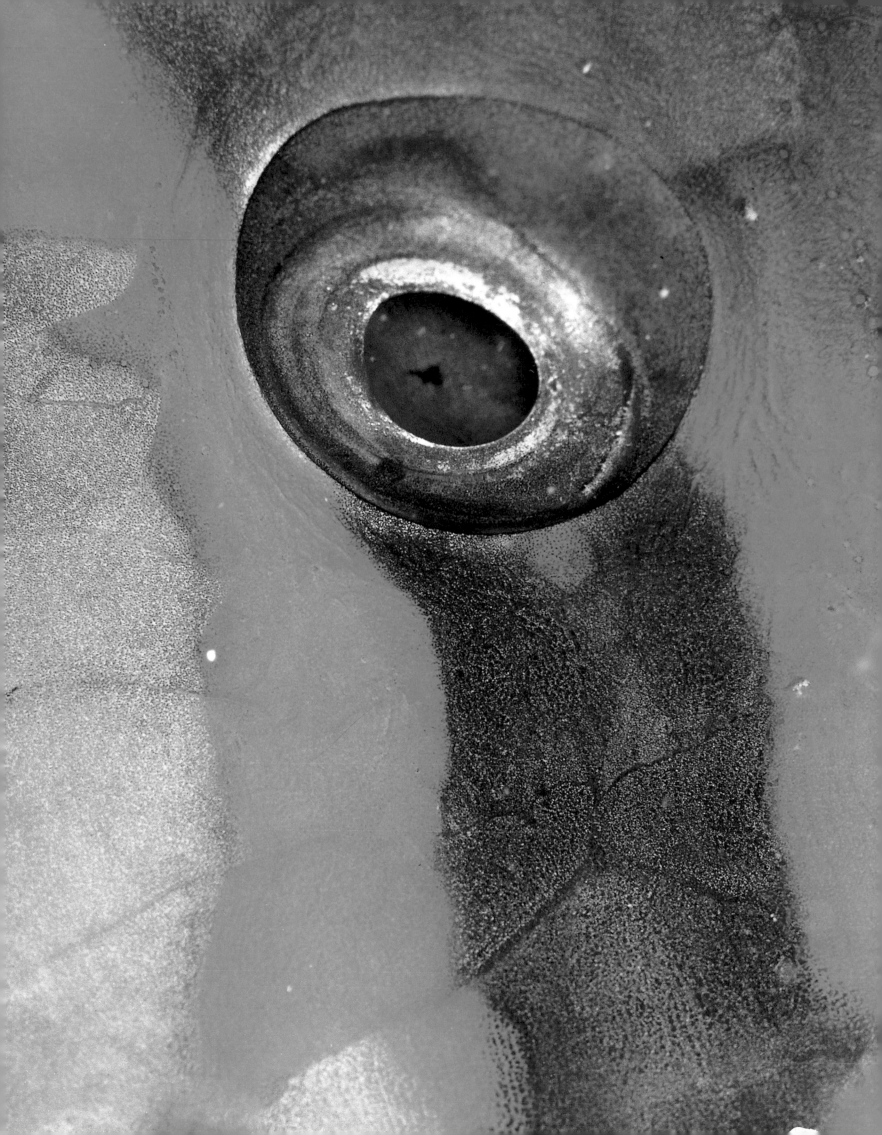

for Alkistis

Realm of the Pygmy Seahorse

An Underwater Photography Adventure

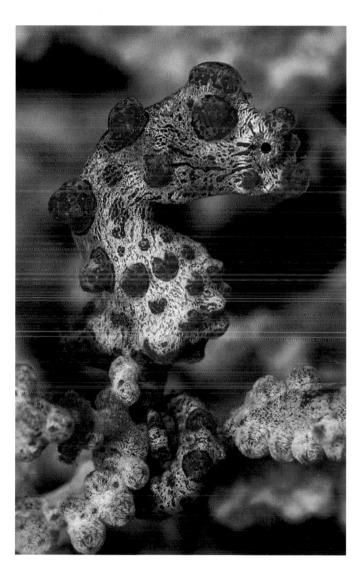

Photographs & Text by

Constantinos Petrinos

Starfish Press

Published by
Starfish Press
23 Spetson Str, Athens 15342, Greece

Photographs & Text
© 2001, 2002 CONSTANTINOS PETRINOS

e-mail info@petrinos.gr
website www.petrinos.gr

Design & Project Management
Creators Publications Ltd
www.creators.gr

Text Editor
Caroline Taggart

Colour Scanning
Première Digital
www.PremiereDesign.co.uk

Colour Reproduction
Next S.A.
Athens, Greece

Printing & Binding
Andreou S.A.
www.andreu.gr

ISBN 960-87016-0-0

Scientific Editor
David W. Behrens

Page 2:
This minuscule unidentified crab on a sea urchin
Astropyga radiata was barely visible.

Page 4:
Zebra lionfish, Dendrochirus zebra (20cm).
Pectoral fin detail.

Page 7:
Juvenile Volitans lionfish, Pterois volitans (38cm).

Page 9:
The coral shrimp, Vir philippinensis (1.5cm), is
found only in association with bubble coral,
usually with Plerogyra sinuosa, as in this picture.
Plerogyra expands during the day to expose the
symbiotic algae in its tissue to sunlight. At night the
polyps shrink and droop, which is why few divers
ever see bubble coral at night.

FOREWORD
BY THE SCIENTIFIC EDITOR

Each and every one of us has a different reason for running off to our favourite underwater hideaway. For some it is escape, or relaxation, or maybe even therapy. For others it is to fulfil an innate desire to see and learn about the fascinating oddities that live and prosper in an environment where we are foreigners, an environment we cannot even enter without a face mask to see and a tank of air to breathe.

Those of us fortunate enough to be able to dive in this magical world go through an interesting routine each time we step off that boat or beach into the warm, clear waters. This routine usually includes clearing our regulator, adjusting our face mask, monkeying with our BCD and, if we carry a camera, making last minute checks of strobes and focus.

Once this dance is complete and we look downward in advance of our descent, we are almost always taken by the overwhelming grandeur and diversity of the seascape ahead. I have asked many of my dive partners to estimate the number of species in their field of view. The answer is usually the same – 'Oh, a dozen or two.' This is where Constantinos and I get excited and jump on our bandwagon to show you that if you look closer, you will quickly learn that your 'dozen or two' estimate is off by an order of magnitude. A more accurate estimate would be 'a couple of hundred'. Those of you who reply with an emphatic 'No way!' will be thoroughly amazed at what Constantinos offers us here.

The following pages are proof of what can be discovered by slowing down, looking closer and being one with the details of the seascape. Constantinos takes us by the hand and introduces us to what he sees. To say that a whole new world unfolds is an understatement. That which first appears as simply a large colourful coral head now reveals dozens of inhabitants and relationships, previously overlooked in our haste to get to that next beautiful coral head beyond. That so many animal species can live together, some commensally, some competitively, will open an entire new vista for you in the sport you already enjoy.

Constantinos's underwater sojourns will introduce you to what many of us refer to as the fascinating 'muck' dive, an experience you will want to repeat over and over again. Little could we imagine that there was so much to discover by swimming away from the brightly coloured creations blossoming from the patch reef, and venturing out over sand bottoms, often in areas where the visibility wanes from that boasted in vacation resort brochures. It is here that true discovery lies waiting. It is the muck dive that will treat you to Constantinos's bobtail squid and the amazing wonderpus.

Whether crawling or swimming among the delicate and graceful branches of a gorgeous dendronephid soft coral, or ambling out on a dark coral sand bottom, amazing animals, displaying amazing features, colours and behaviours are yours. You will find the rewards so great that you will have difficulty sharing them with your friends.

Constantinos has studied this amazing and diverse corner of our globe with the hope of documenting and sharing its many wonderful inhabitants. He has done so without causing harm or disrespect to a single creature. If he can find, observe and enjoy such detail and so many tiny miracles, then so can you.

For the diver, Constantinos's masterpiece will excite and inspire you before your next trip, giving you ideas of what to look for and how to make that next, really great discovery, while also offering a souvenir of your trip once it is over, to tickle the memory of things you saw and moments you experienced.

For the non-diver, the coral reef admirer, this book documents the most valuable environmental heritage we have. It is a testimonial to the importance of a self-sustaining microcosm, a reminder of what you and I can leave for our children and theirs, if we respect and protect the oceans.

Read Constantinos's words, enjoy his spectacular photographs and revel in the gift of discovery he is offering to share with us.

David W. Behrens
Author of *Coral Reef Animals of the Indo-Pacific*
Danville, California, USA

FOREWORD

The first time I met Constantinos Petrinos I was called back to my office from a meeting by a senior editor saying I *must* see this photographer's work. She wasn't wrong. The work was staggering – and incidentally it was all from the Lembeh Strait.

At *Dive* magazine we see hundreds of sets of underwater photographs each year and few stand out. But even on the most cursory examination of the images on the light box it was clear these were special and as I looked more closely and spoke to Constantinos I realised that a rare talent had wandered into our offices.

Not only could he take graphically beautiful photographs, but he understood his subjects intimately. Far too often those with the scientific knowledge and curiosity lack the artistic eye. And Constantinos's enthusiasm and excitement about the marine world were palpable. The images captured unique and fascinating behaviour under the sea – those defining moments which can take hours and hours of patient preparation and those lucky shots when only the knowledgeable know the right time to hit the shutter.

Since then Constantinos has spent even more time searching for weird critters in Lembeh and the results are outstanding. This book takes you on a fabulous journey and shows aspects of the underwater world which only a very few have been privileged to see.

Graeme Gourlay
Publisher of *Dive* and *Oceans Illustrated* magazines
Richmond, Surrey, England

The Lembeh Strait Preservation Society was established in 1997 with one single mission: to safeguard and preserve the unique biodiversity of the Lembeh area. Towards this mission, our primary objective is to establish a National Marine Park and then assist the local government in running it. Of course, educating the various people involved – local fishermen, government officials, students and tourists – is a primary means in achieving these objectives. Photographs speak a thousand words and, for the first time, we have in our hands an outstanding book, whose excellent photographs will be an invaluable tool in showing the people concerned the unique marine wonders of the Lembeh area and convincing them to do their share in preserving it for future generations.

It is in this context that I am pleased to introduce this book to you. Enjoy its fascinating photographs and 'travel' with them to the Lembeh Strait. We, on the other hand, will continue to treasure this incomparable underwater wonderland, and hope that you will decide to experience it yourselves someday. Until then, *Salam sejahtera*.

Captain R.W. Billy Matindas, M.Sc.
Chairman of the Lembeh Strait Preservation Society
Sulawesi, Indonesia

CONTENTS

Introduction
12

Photography & Conservation
30

The Coral Reef
44

Survival Recipes
68

Innovative Housing Concepts
104

Reef Sex
136

Crinoid Community
152

Snails & Nudibranchs
160

Seahorses & Pipefishes
182

Fishes
194

Epilogue
240

Notes & Abbreviations
244

Acknowledgements
248

References
252

Index to Photographs
256

THAILAND

SOUTH CHINA SEA

BRUNEI

MALAYSIA

MALAYSIA

SINGAPORE

Sumatra

Borneo

INDIAN
OCEAN

JAVA SEA

Jakarta

I N D O

Java

Bali

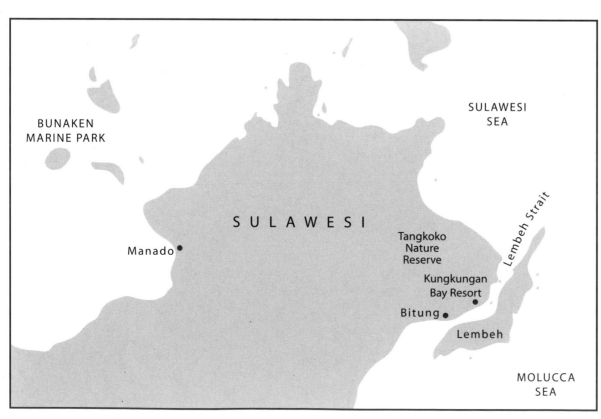

BUNAKEN
MARINE PARK

SULAWESI
SEA

S U L A W E S I

Lembeh Strait

Manado

Tangkoko
Nature
Reserve

Kungkungan
Bay Resort

Bitung

Lembeh

MOLUCCA
SEA

PACIFIC
OCEAN

SULAWESI SEA

Manado •

*MOLUCCA
SEA*

Sulawesi

*BANDA
SEA*

Ujung
Pandang •

N E S I A

Irian Jaya

FLORES SEA

Timor

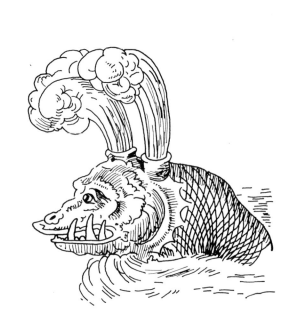

*The Indonesian Archipelago is normally said to
comprise 13,677 islands. In fact, some surveys
estimate as many as 18,500 and no one really
knows the exact number. Early mariners associated
these uncharted waters with sea monsters. Indonesia
is about three times the size of Texas. Sumatra is
comparable to Sweden, Sulawesi to Great Britain
and Java to California. New Guinea and Borneo
are the second and third islands in the world after
Greenland. With a total land area of two million
sq. km, Indonesia is the fourteenth largest country
in the world.*

INTRODUCTION

Indonesia has a population of 210 million people, making it the world's fourth most populous nation after China, India and the USA. This population is very unevenly distributed, with 60% of Indonesians (about 125 million people) living on the island of Java, which has a population density more than twice that of Japan. The Indonesian Archipelago is normally said to comprise 13,677 islands. In fact, some surveys estimate as many as 18,500 and no one really knows the exact number. About 6,000 islands are named and 1000 are inhabited. If you were to move Indonesia over the map, it would stretch from Boston to London.

Development of the area began in the 16th century, when European spice traders realised the importance of these islands. During much of the 17th and 18th centuries, the Dutch East India Company had a trade monopoly here, in the area then known as the East Indies. The islands supplied most of the world's quinine and pepper, over a third of its rubber, a quarter of its coconut products and almost a fifth of its tea, sugar, coffee and oil. The exploitation of these natural resources turned the Netherlands into a major colonial power and contributed to its industrialisation. In the 19th century, the Dutch focused their colonial efforts on the fertile fields of Java, leading to the island's population explosion.

Dutch rule continued until the time of the Second World War, when Indonesia was occupied by the Japanese. Then, on August 17 1945, Indonesia's first president, Sukarno, declared independence. The Dutch were unwilling to surrender their colony, and the ensuing wars cost the lives of thousands of Indonesians. In Southern Sulawesi alone, Captain Raymond Westerling's special troops are said to have killed 40,000 Indonesians in a desperate attempt to control the region. In July 1947, the Dutch launched a major offensive, which led to a United Nations intervention. After a further two years of conflict, the colonists finally left on December 27 1949.

Today, there are approximately 300 ethnic groups in Indonesia speaking some 365 languages and dialects. The official language is Bahasa Indonesian, a variant of Malay which was used in the spice trade. Indonesia is the largest Islamic nation in the world, with significant Christian and Hindu minorities and a fascinating variety of cultures. Its land and waters exhibit a similar diversity in landscape and in flora and fauna. This is all part of the spectacular Indonesian experience!

For millennia, climatological and geological processes created the necessary conditions for the tropical Indo-Pacific to evolve into the most diverse area among marine ecosystems. The Indonesian-Philippines area is the epicentre of this amazing biodiversity, which decreases in gradient as we move further away.

For decades, diving in Indonesia was synonymous with the islands of Sulawesi and Bali. In North Sulawesi, Manado and the Bunaken Marine Park, with its clear waters and spectacular walls, attracted hundreds of divers. The Lembeh Strait remained a well-kept secret, despite the fact that it is only a short one-hour drive towards the northeastern tip of Sulawesi. There, the busy port city of Bitung is the centre of economic activity. Facing it is Lembeh Island. The strait that forms between Lembeh and the Sulawesi mainland is 16km long and 1-2km wide.

This page: Funerary figures, Tana Toraja, central Sulawesi.

Opposite: Rice fields in central Sulawesi.

Kungkungan Bay Resort house reef at low tide.

Typical Kungkungan Bay Resort guesthouse in the local architectural style.

Fortunately for divers, in 1989, two friends, Kathryn Ecenbarger and the late Helen Staples, sailed through the Lembeh Strait and it was love at first sight. An old coconut plantation was purchased on the Sulawesi coast of the strait and Mark Ecenbarger, Kathryn's son, undertook to realise the dreams of the two ladies. Kungkungan Bay Resort (KBR) was born and Sulawesi was rediscovered. The resort immediately attracted big names in underwater photography. Scientists arrived in search of new species and film crews chased after elusive animals. Today, it is simply impossible to keep track of the numerous articles in magazines all over the world that tell of the weird and wonderful marine creatures of the Lembeh Strait.

KBR is an exceptional case study in resort development. Those who conceived it wished to avoid the mistakes that had led to overexploitation elsewhere, forever altering formerly pristine dive destinations. They were determined not to place an excessive burden on the ecosystem. Massive dive tourism, although a lucrative business option, was to be excluded. Preservation, rather than exploitation for a quick profit, became KBR's philosophy. Instead of erecting a large hotel complex, they opted for a small-scale development, with the added benefit of the charm of the traditional Minahasan architecture. Only 12 luxury guesthouses were built, together with a central restaurant and administration building. There are four boats and a maximum of eight diving guests is allowed per dive site. As a result, there is minimum diver pressure. Long-term preservation is a constant concern. For this purpose, KBR co-operates with government agencies, as well as local and international conservation societies. A major goal is to achieve marine park status for the area.

Lembeh Strait is ideal for year-round diving. The mountains of mainland Sulawesi to the west and those of Lembeh Island to the east protect the strait from the seasonal monsoons. The dive sites have a variety of habitats. Seemingly barren volcanic sand slopes and rubble areas reveal elusive, rare creatures, such as the wonderpus and the mimic octopus. Tiny pygmy seahorses adorn *Muricella* sea fans. Spectacular nudibranchs are everywhere. The rare and unusual seem commonplace. Here is an entry from my logbook:

'The incredible concentration of frogfishes at Makawide explains why the Lembeh Strait is often called the 'Frogfish Capital of the World'. The place is littered with them to such a point that after a while one tends to ignore them, just like the many puffers at Hairball. There is a big (25cm) yellow frogfish near the mooring; a marble-coloured one on a mushroom leather coral further away and a cluster of four frogfishes at the 10-12m range. A total of six frogfishes in a relatively small area is quite incredible. Note: Dive again tomorrow. Check for additional frogfishes that I could not spot.'

In the 1960s and 1970s, the Lembeh Strait was a major migration highway for large pelagics such as whale sharks and manta rays. Marine biologist Silvester Benny Pratasik told me that he can still remember the profusion of sharks and turtles that cruised the waters when he was a child. Even in the early 1980s, these creatures were seen regularly. Indeed, if it were not for overfishing, the unique geographical position of the Lembeh Strait would make it both a big animal destination and an important location for macro photography. For millennia, the rich supply of plankton in the strait sustained a highly diverse ecosystem, from tiny plankton-feeding invertebrates to huge whale sharks. It took only a decade of overfishing to wipe out the pelagics. A few years ago, some KBR guests had the opportunity to swim for about 20 minutes with a whale shark that was passing right in front of the resort, but this is rare. Today, the Lembeh Strait is a dream dive destination for its unusual benthic animals – those that live on the ocean floor – but not for the pelagics.

Kungkungan Bay showing the KBR restaurant and administration building and the dive boat pier.

This book aims to reveal the marine wonders of the Lembeh Strait and hopefully make us all more conscious of the marine environment. Obviously, the project was a tremendous learning experience for me. I hope that divers will use this book to prepare themselves before visiting Lembeh or, indeed, any coral reef in the Indo-Pacific. Moreover, the book may be attractive to nature lovers, environmentally aware readers and anyone who shares the joy of discovering the wonders of this world. My personal aspiration is for the book to become a tool that will assist the organisations working towards the establishment of a marine park in the area.

Over the years, the Lembeh Strait has become my favourite dive destination. Once the book project was conceived, I spent months preparing my equipment and studying. The core expedition lasted five months. During those months, I did 320 dives and produced 25,000 slides.

GENERAL INFORMATION

The Lembeh Strait is surprisingly easy to get to. Simply take one of the many flights to Singapore. A three-and-a-half-hour connecting flight will take you to Manado International Airport in North Sulawesi. An English-speaking member of KBR's staff will greet you at the airport and escort you on the hour-long drive to the resort. The climate is tropical with a gentle ocean breeze throughout the year. Temperatures are around 30°C/85°F during the day and 25°C/75°F at night. For diving, a 3mm wetsuit is all you need. There are four scheduled boat dives per day, as well as optional beac dives. The latter are scheduled only after consulting the dive manager. A big camera room is conveniently located facing the KBR pier. There is plenty of space to set up your equipment. There are 220V and 110V battery charge stations.

When is a good time to go diving in the Lembeh Strait? I would say any time. I chose the low season (December-April) for all my trips and I had a great time. The visibility is not as good as it is during the high season (May-November) but do not forget that this is the macro photography Mecca of the world and you will not be shooting much wide angle anyway. The resort's small size guarantees that you will never have crowded dive sites. As a rule, for most dive destinations, it is the 'good season criterion' that dictates travel plans. I believe that as far as the Lembeh Strait is concerned, the 'good season criterion' comes second. You can plan your dive vacation when it suits you best and still enjoy yourself enormously. Lonely Planet's Indonesian guide book and *Underwater Indonesia* by Karl Muller are indispensable in preparing for your trip. Check out visa requirements and health precautions well in advance.

REGIONAL ATTRACTIONS

The resort can arrange short trips for those who want to explore North Sulawesi. Visitors are escorted by KBR staff members, who act as guides and interpreters. I highly recommend the early morning trip to the fish and vegetable markets of Bitung. The markets are bustling with activity and the people are extremely friendly. Bitung is a busy port and north Sulawesi has a long tradition in trade. The people are used to coming in contact with other cultures. Westerners are sometimes distant, perhaps because they do not speak the language. However, I found that an integral part of the learning experience is communicating with the people. Using my limited Bahasa Indonesian vocabulary and assisted by the KBR staff, I was able to make friends with local produce sellers. Since these early morning trips did not involve a sacrifice of diving time, I visited the markets whenever a trip was scheduled. I enjoyed the interaction with the people and acquired a wealth of information from my guide, usually Atriantje or Merlyn from the restaurant staff. On the topic of culinary preferences, Merlyn confessed that she considers cooked dog an irresistible delicacy, whereas Atriantje prefers beef.

Opposite: This is a farmer's kid assisting his father planting rice. Despite his youth, he was working in knee high mud with the fervour of an adult. Leeches and attacks by swarms of malarial mosquitoes is the curse of the rice paddies. The photo was taken when the boy went to fetch their lunch box.

Overleaf left: During one of my many visits to the fish market in Bitung, we went at 5.30 a.m. to watch the big fishing boats coming in. This young boy jumped in the water to straighten the nets. As the early morning light hit him, I felt a great reverence for the capacity of one so young to cope with a much tougher life than mine.

Overleaf right: Kids all over the world love to chew bubblegum, climb trees or simply stare at strangers.

Unlike other parts of the world, the merchants will not pester you to buy something. However, this is part of the fun. I bought so many hot red peppers from my favourite seller that I would have spontaneously combusted had I actually consumed them. But it was great to drop by, ask how business was going and buy something. I was curious as to why many people were even friendlier when I told them that I was *Yunan*, Greek. I should have known better. Quite a few of the people I met at the port had worked for Greek shipowners.

If you are a superfit gym resident, you should climb the extinct volcano Manado Tua that dominates the landscape northeast of the capital. My system has a natural tendency to abort long climbs, so I have never joined this excursion. However, I am told that if you reach the top on a clear day, you will be rewarded by a spectacular panoramic view of the Manado Bay islands.

In Sawangan, 24km from Manado, there is an ancient Minahasan cemetery that is well worth a visit. It contains 144 sarcophagi called *waruga*, dating from as early as the 9th century. These square stone tombs have a burial chamber in the middle and a prism-shaped cover. Each *waruga* is adorned with decorative sculpture and carvings, denoting the characteristics, occupation or cause of death of the deceased. They all have an eastern orientation, towards the rising sun.

Beyond Sawangan, the narrow winding road follows the course of the Tondano River. This scenic trip will take you to the highlands and Lake Tondano, 36km southwest of Manado and 700m above sea level. A stopover at the small town of Tomohon (City of Flowers) is highly recommended. The city lies between two volcanoes, Lokon and Mahawu. The delightfully temperate climate is ideal for fruits and gorgeous flowers – bougainvilleas, gladioli, hibiscus and irises. The Tomohon market is much bigger than the one in Bitung and the food items more diverse. There are colourful flowers and Minahasan culinary exotica, such as fruit bats, dogs and field rats. Note that the market operates only on Tuesday, Thursday and Saturday mornings. Bukit Inspirasi (Inspirational Hill) will give you a spectacular view of the town and the two volcanoes. These short excursions will take you through rice paddies and make your Sulawesi experience more complete. I strongly recommend Karl Muller's *Sulawesi – Island Crossroads of Indonesia* if you are seeking attractions of specialist interest.

A tour of the rainforest should not be missed. You will have the chance to see some of Sulawesi's unique animals and plants. You could schedule a one-day tour for your last non-diving day before your flight home. The Tangkoko Nature Reserve is only a 90-minute ride from KBR. In the beach forest, you can see the world's largest concentration of black-crested macaques, *Macaca nigra*, in social groups that may comprise as many as 100 individuals. A professional rainforest ranger will take you to see the world's smallest primate, the tarsier, *Tarsius spectrum*. It is the size of a rat (about 12cm long) and weighs about 200g. This will definitely be the highlight of your rainforest experience. Tarsiers are nocturnal and hide among dense vegetation or tree hollows during the daytime. Your guide will probably take you to a particular tree in the reserve that houses a community of these gremlin-like creatures. As dusk falls, you will see them emerging from the hollows of their residence to feed on insects. They have large eyes and bat-like ears that move independently of one another. A weak flashlight is necessary to view the tarsiers. Because they have extremely sensitive eyes, you should not shine your flashlight directly into their face. It bothers them, the same way it bothers you during night dives. If you take flash photography, do not bombard a single individual with your flashgun. There will be plenty of opportunities for photography.

Scenes from the fruit, vegetable and fish markets, Bitung, where I liked to go and socialise when I wasn't diving.

Overleaf: Working in the rice fields.

Funerary figures, Tana Toraja, central Sulawesi.

Tangkoko is also famous for its endemic red-knobbed hornbills, *Phyticeros cassidix*. They emit raucous barks as they fly over the rainforest canopy. The park rangers know the trees they frequent and their nest sites during the July-January breeding season. During their stay at KBR, one Swiss family, the Haldis, saw six pairs of hornbills in a single afternoon, which is testimony to the fact that Tangkoko has the highest density in the world for forest hornbills. I decided that this was the time to skip a day's diving and devote a day to photographing these spectacular birds. Unfortunately, the night before my arrival at the park, it rained a lot. Therefore, during my gruesome morning trek, which lasted five hours, the only animal I was able to see and photograph was a cricket. So much for hornbills. I felt like a fool taking my heavy 600mm lens, tripod and camera bag for a ride in the rainforest. However, my luck changed during the four-hour-long afternoon trek. The ranger tracked a hornbill pair sitting on a tree in a perfect position. I was able to set up my tripod and fire off several ASA 400 speed films. Unfortunately, all my Tangkoko films were destroyed in an ill-fated courier shipment. During my subsequent trip to the rainforest, I was so demoralised by the film loss that I only joined the dusk tour to photograph the tarsiers.

Long pants, trekking boots and insect repellent are imperative for this highly recommended rainforest trip, and a flashlight is essential on the dusk tour.

Dive Planning

The project required intensive diving over a significant length of time. I was aware that long repetitive dives over an extended period fall outside the norms of computer-assisted diving. Therefore, I scheduled a day off once a week to allow my tissues to desaturate. For every dive, I kept a detailed description of the dive profile, the dive route and the marine life. I drew maps for every dive site and marked the location of attractive habitats, for example a sponge outcrop, which I checked regularly.

I may have done some weird things, but overall, I have been a 'good boy' most of the time. I would, however, like to mention an amusing incident. I am a night-dive fanatic, which led my friends at KBR to name me Con (Creature of the Night). The KBR house reef was my favourite night-dive spot. One day I decided to go for a dive at 7 p.m. I stayed under the pier and never went deeper than 8m. I had four cameras on the bottom and was getting some good shots. I kept going in and out, changing film and lenses and experimenting in the shallows. At 11 p.m., my exhausted dive guide had to go home. I reluctantly emerged from the water and had started dismantling my equipment when I thought, 'I can't go to bed this early!' I put on a new tank and snuck quietly underwater. I was in heaven once again. At about midnight, I had found a huge lobster at the coral head under the pier (depth 4m) and was working on it with an assortment of lenses. Unfortunately, the resort's owner, Mark Ecenbarger, happened to be on his way to bed and could not help but notice the 'Kuwait air-raid' that was taking place right under his pier! He had no difficulty in guessing who it was, and he immediately called on the security guard on duty to log my activities and report to him in the morning. I was in deep trouble next day because, apparently, I had got a little carried away and had not left the water until 1.30 a.m. For some reason, after that night, my equipment was locked up after 11 o'clock. Mark is a good friend, but this was really unfair!

Tarsier, Tarsius spectrum (12cm).

Javan pond-heron, Ardeola speciosa.

Brown dottybacks, Pseudochromis fuscus (9cm), engaged in a territorial fight. The fighting took place under a rock in about 3m of water, right next to our boat's mooring at Pintu Colada. The rock seemed rather uninteresting to me and there was no dearth of rocks in the area to justify such a fuss. On the other hand, humans have been fighting for centuries over pieces of rock and I am sure that fish do not understand that either… The fighting went on for about 15 seconds and, eventually, the fish on the right, apparently the bigger of the two, won.

I have juxtaposed these two pictures to show the sharp contrast between the striking colours of a typical coral reef and the monochromatic background of a muck dive site. On this page, there is a pair of cockatoo waspfish, Ablabys taenianotus (15cm), in a muck dive site in the Lembeh Strait. It is rare that two waspfish are found together in the wild. Aggregations of Inimicus species are more common. Species of this genus appear to aggregate inshore seasonally, probably for reproduction.

Opposite: Orange anthias, Pseudanthias squamipinnis (15cm), hovering in the current in a colourful coral reef in Fiji. The females are orange and the larger males are purplish.

My life above and below the water was quite eventful. One day, I fell on the boat and, in my attempt to save my camera, cracked one of my ribs. Needless to say, I did not stop diving. It was painful and probably foolish, but at the time I thought that I could not afford to stay out of the water. My land photography was even more adventurous. While kneeling on the ground to photograph a beetle, I sat on top of a termite mound. As I was concentrating on the photography, I did not realise that I was soon covered with termites. They started biting me everywhere, including my scalp, face and lips. I dropped my Nikon F5 on the ground and started running for the sea, remembering at the last minute that I had a 'cheap' lens in my pocket, which I tossed in perfect style into a flower pot. I jumped into the water fully dressed, right in front of the restaurant. The guests probably thought this was part of the resort's in-house entertainment.

KBR Dive Guides

Although I am certainly biased by my friendship with them, it is not an exaggeration to say that these are perhaps the best dive buddies I have ever had. For several years now, Kungkungan Bay Resort has been in the spotlight because of the unique qualities of the Lembeh Strait and the biodiversity of the region. Apart from the extensive training provided by the resort, the dive guides have acquired invaluable experience through guiding the countless underwater photographers, marine biologists and film crews who have visited the strait. You do not have to be a professional to appreciate their expertise. The strait is full of creatures which use camouflage to blend with the environment. As a result, they are truly invisible to the untrained eye. This is irrespective of one's dive experience. As a visiting diver, one needs time to adjust and perceive a new marine environment and its inhabitants. The KBR dive guides are the key professionals who will reveal the marine wonders of the area and make your dives memorable.

A word of caution. The Lembeh Strait has very strong currents. This does not represent a problem for dive scheduling since there are over 30 dive sites along the Strait. The dive manager at KBR decides on the dive site, basing his judgement on tide charts issued by the Indonesian Maritime Authority. However, the final decision on whether to dive a particular site rests with the dive guide, who will evaluate the condition of the current in situ. It is recommended to carry along a 'sausage' (surface marker). In fact, I would suggest that you make this a standard practice for any dive trip.

Dive Sites

The more than 30 dive sites which have so far been explored and established by the KBR dive team include three wrecks that have evolved into outstanding coral reefs. The management discourages wreck penetration and collection of wreck items. Fixed moorings have been set at all sites to avoid having to throw an anchor over the reef. The dive guides use secret landmarks to find the submerged mooring buoys – buoys left on the surface would be co-opted as anchorage by subsistence fishermen. The dive team monitors the dive sites and the moorings regularly. All the sites are given names, and I have occasionally mentioned these in the text – for clarity, I have put their names in italics. There is even a site which the dive team calls *Con's Reef* in honour of our friendship and the good times we have had together.

This page: The lush vegetation of KBR gardens is ideal for land photography in between dives.

Opposite: Zebra lionfish, Dendrochirus zebra (18cm), hiding inside a barrel sponge.

PHOTOGRAPHY & CONSERVATION

The combination of salt water and electronic cameras is the Devil's playground!
Fred Bavendam

The purpose of this book is not to teach you underwater photography. There are excellent books that cover the techniques from various perspectives. However, the following are a few guidelines on the way that I work underwater.

Some readers like to see the f-stop and shutter speed associated with each photograph. I decided to omit this information, not for fear of disclosing any precious secret, but because I believe it is useless. The aperture/shutter speed combination depends on a number of factors such as the distance from the camera to the subject, strobe power and available light. You simply cannot rely on a rule of thumb and apply the same camera settings irrespective of the variables of the particular photograph. Instead, I suggest you familiarise yourself thoroughly with your equipment before a trip. A swimming pool is an ideal environment in which to do your test rolls. You can shoot and compare several rolls of film under almost identical conditions. For this purpose, some photographers sink plastic fish in a swimming pool.

The gross weight of the equipment I used on my five-month trip was exactly 220 kilos and it was transported courtesy of Singapore Airlines and Silkair. The film in itself weighed 20 kilos. Planning such a long stay without any assistants was a logistics nightmare. I had to make sure that I had multiple back-ups of every single item and, despite months of planning, several pieces of equipment (additional Ultralight arms, extra cameras and lenses) had to be airmailed to satisfy photographic requirements that arose as a result of conditions I discovered on location. My room became a spare parts heaven for other KBR guests.

I used four cameras for most of my dives. My primary systems were two Nikon F4 cameras in Subal underwater housings, and my secondary, two Nikonos RS cameras. I used nine Nikon SB-105 and two Nikon SB-104 strobes. The cameras were numbered. I usually left them on the sand and retrieved them when necessary, or asked the dive guide to bring me the appropriate number. On several occasions I lost a camera. The dive guides quickly became accustomed to my panicked looks and organised salvage operations when needed. On one occasion, Fred Bavendam spent more than an hour snorkelling, trying to find the Nikonos RS camera that I had expertly hidden on a rubble slope.

Given the nature of the marine environment in the Lembeh Strait, you are likely to spend most of your vacation doing macro photography. The wide-angle opportunities are limited. If you are serious about close-up photography, you cannot rely on framers to achieve the best results. Extension tubes and framers work well with either Nikonos or Sea & Sea cameras and will give you acceptable results for souvenir photos, but getting razor-sharp images is not easy. In addition, a framer allows you to photograph only co-operative subjects such as soft corals or nudibranchs. Any attempt to photograph skittish subjects, such as gobies, will prove futile. Therefore, a housed system is imperative. Although most manufacturers produce housings exclusively for Nikon cameras, some Canon housings have also started to appear on the market.

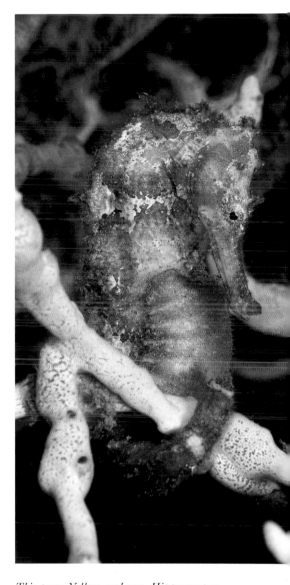

This page: Yellow seahorse, Hippocampus kuda, (17cm).

Opposite: Painted frogfish, Antennarius pictus (10cm).

Regarding lens selection, Nikon's AF 105mm f/2.8 D Micro lens is what you need for the majority of macro shots. In Lembeh, I occasionally used the bulkier and heavier AF 200mm f/4 D Micro lens, when I needed to photograph a particularly shy subject that would not allow me to get within the 105mm's range. The 200mm lens doubles the working distance and allowed me to get a similar picture to that of the 105mm, while being positioned twice as far from the subject. The 200mm lens comes with a tripod collar, which prevents it fitting inside the housing port. However, it is easy to have the collar removed at a Nikon service centre so that it fits inside the port without a problem.

When photographing particularly small subjects, I sometimes used a +1 or +2 dioptre close-up lens for extra magnification. For twice life-size shots, I used a 2x teleconverter with the 105mm lens. Although this increases magnification dramatically, there is a significant loss in depth of field. A few pictures in this book were shot using this set-up. Many others ended up in the wastebasket.

A good strobe is useless unless you can position it exactly where you want it. This is definitely not the case with rigid arms, which limit strobe positioning. My preference is for Ultralight Control Systems, a company which produces high-quality modular strobe arms and camera trays. The material used – aluminium – and the design ensure that the arms are lightweight. Strobe arms come in various lengths. I prefer short arms for macro, to streamline my camera system as much as possible. For wide angle, I use longer arms to position the strobes further away from the camera. I do not usually handhold my strobes. If you choose to do so, make sure that the arm does not end up becoming a support stick.

A camera system is an underwater photographer's most valued possession. It represents significant expenditure and, if lost, cannot be replaced instantly. It is, therefore, understandable that some photographers try to find ways to attach their beloved outfit securely to either their BCD or their wrist, using a lanyard. In my opinion, this can prove fatal in an emergency. I have not seen many photographers dropping their cameras. After all, a camera receives a photographer's undivided attention. The only time you would drop it is during an emergency, usually while trying to assist someone else. Later, when everything is under control, you will probably be able to retrieve it intact from the bottom. Even if you were to lose the outfit, there can be no comparison between the value of your camera and that of your buddy. A camera system hanging from your BCD could seriously hamper your ability to provide assistance. Personally, I do not use a lanyard even on blue-water dives, for example to photograph dolphins, where there is no chance of retrieval.

During my trips to the Lembeh Strait, I ruined two F4 cameras. The first flooded when I decided to dive without closing the back of my Subal housing. I did not win the stupidity award that year, so I tried harder on my next trip.

The Conspiracy: Packing 220 kilos of equipment was a nightmare. I did my last morning dive, washed my gear, hung my wetsuit, BCD and other paraphernalia in the sun and headed to the restaurant to trim my waistline with some great churros. Nuswanto, the chief supervisor of the dive team, approached me with a smile.

This page: Mushroom coral detail, Fungia fungites (28cm). Photographing patterns is easy and the result is usually aesthetically pleasing.

Opposite: Polycerid nudibranch, Thecacera picta (1cm).

'Mr Con, guess what I found at *Aw Shucks*?'

'The mooring? Good for you, Nus,' I remarked without stopping.

Undaunted by my sarcasm, Nus followed after me.

'But, Mr Con…'

'Nus, do you realise you are keeping me from a very urgent churros mission?'

'Oh, okay. I just thought you might like to know that what I found was a new crinoid shrimp.'

Now it was my turn to start running after him.

'What? Nus! Please help me assemble my gear! We're diving *Aw Shucks* right away!'

The next day, I started washing my gear once again. Packing for a second time proved to be a horrible experience, but by 5 p.m. I was almost done. When the dive boats came in from the afternoon dive, I could not resist the temptation to go and meet them. Wilson, one of the supervisors, informed me that they had seen yet another amazing crinoid shrimp.

'It looked like a zebra. The guests where very happy and Mr Ken took *banyak* [many] photos!'

The shrimp had been sighted at *Nudi Falls*, at a depth of 3m. How could I resist? I had to take everything out of the suitcases and assemble my dive and camera gear again. I decided to take two Subal F4 camera housings: one with the 105mm lens and another with the 105mm lens and a 2x teleconverter. Within 45 minutes I was cruising with Wilson and Dante towards *Nudi Falls*. Wilson tied the mooring and I hit the water in zero time. Dante gave me the two cameras and I started the dive. Seconds later, I shot to the surface shouting, 'Flood!' Dante dove instantly, grabbed my Subal swimming pool and brought it on to the boat.

'Thank you, Dante. How much water?'

'*Banyak*.'

I did not need to see the mess to know that the Nikon F4, the 105mm lens and the 2x teleconverter were history. But I still had a housing with the 105mm lens to complete my shooting. Wilson was already near the *Nudi Falls* wall and I joined him. Indeed, the crinoid shrimp was spectacular and I finished my roll. Back at the resort, I tossed my Nikon F4 camera and lens into the wastebasket and started packing again. That crinoid shrimp was certainly a new species: at US$4500, it was the most expensive crinoid shrimp ever photographed! This flood had occurred because of my rush to set up the housing. When I closed the front port, the O-ring had twisted and gone outside the O-ring groove.

Many divers ask me how often I greased my O-rings. In general, I adhere to the principle, 'If it has not flooded, do not mess with it.' Not long ago, I was one of those divers who greased all O-rings between dives. However, if you dive with a housing and it does not flood, you know you have a proper seal. Personally, I only checked the O-ring in the back when I had to open the housing to change film. I performed general O-ring maintenance every 10-15 days.

Overall, despite the rough treatment and almost total lack of maintenance, my camera equipment did not let me down. Everything kept functioning perfectly despite the accumulated salt and sand. For those of you who take better care of your equipment, KBR has two huge camera rinse tanks and a third rinse tank for dive gear.

Throughout my trips I used exclusively rechargeable batteries.

Crinoid shrimp, Periclimenes cf. amboinensis (2.5cm). Photos of crinoid shrimps are rather challenging. The photographer needs patience and repeated dives to the host crinoid until the shrimp is in the right position for the photo.

Crinoid Shrimp, Periclimenes commensalis (1.8cm)

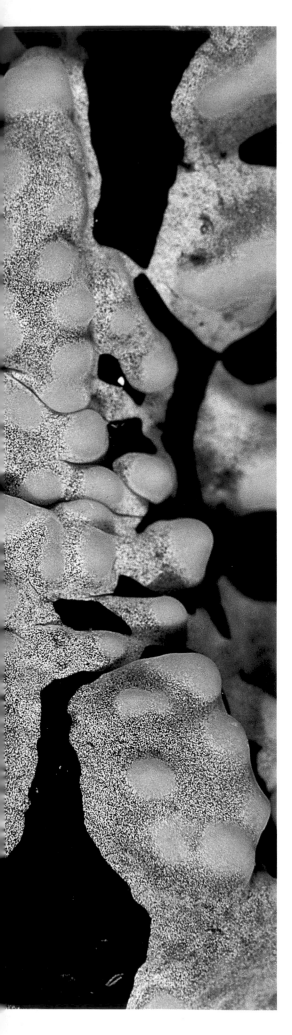

Before You Go

Preparing for a dive trip is half the fun and definitely the key to good photos. I believe I owe much of the success of my pictures to careful preparation. Before a trip my buddy and I spend considerable time reading anything we can find on the behaviour of our subjects. On location, I generally work closely with dive guides who know the area and I follow their advice. This sounds simple, but few people truly capitalise on the dive guides' knowledge. When I first started taking underwater photos, I was very eager to be the first in the water and also the first to take shots of any subject. It took a couple of years for me to realise that such fervour would not get me anywhere. Eventually, I cottoned on to the fact that nobody was going to empty the seas of other underwater photographers just so that I could have *all* the subjects to myself.

Nowadays, I usually let other people get a chance at the shot first. After a couple of frames, they disappear in pursuit of the next great photo opportunity. This allows me to concentrate on the picture I have in mind without being disturbed. Again, in my early days, as soon as I saw a subject, I would rush in to take the shot, any shot. Now, when I find a subject, I immediately move away so that I can examine the situation without causing the animal unnecessary stress. I decide whether I want to take a vertical or horizontal picture and set my strobes accordingly. I then approach very slowly, trying to avoid any sudden movements. This is critical. The subject will interpret the slightest movement in the water as an intrusion by a predator. I usually try to secure a couple of shots first, even if I am further from the subject than I would like. For very skittish subjects, I move back at the slightest sign of apprehension and try again when I think things have settled. Even if I do not have any shots left, I will approach a skittish subject and stay as close as possible for a few minutes. Having gained acceptance, I will return after a suitable surface interval. A good photography course should teach photographers how to approach and leave a site without causing damage to the reef.

Photographers, the author being no exception, sometimes take unnecessary risks, as though a particular photograph will change their lives. Keep in mind that no photograph is worth dying for. This may sound self-evident, but many photographers put their lives at risk. I once met a woman whose father died trying to photograph a jellyfish! He held his breath (a serious scuba-diving safety violation) to take a picture without realising that the jellyfish was ascending. As he came closer to the surface, the air in his lungs expanded, causing a fatal embolism. Practise with your buddy and be meticulous about safety rules.

This page: Skin detail of a phyllidiid nudibranch, Phyllidia sp.

Page 39: This Tozeuma shrimp, Tozeuma armatum (5cm), lives on black coral. Its elongated body and matching colour make it impossible to discern from its host.

Page 40: Porcelain crab on a Scleronephthya soft coral.

Opposite: Crinoid shrimp, Periclimenes commensalis (1.8cm).

CONSERVATION – YOU *can* MAKE A DIFFERENCE

The Indo-Pacific has many marine snails with gorgeous shells. Unfortunately, many end up in tourist markets around the world. The tourist trade has depleted natural stocks to such an extent that nowadays the Philippines and Indonesia are the principal shell suppliers to much of the world. Some end up as decorations, which give an exotic look to cocktail parties and shop windows. Others become promotional items, jewellery or grotesque 'art work'. Collectors around the world pay top prices for the rarer species. You can make a difference if you do not buy seashells or related products. A reduction in demand is the only sound conservation practice. Should you collect an empty shell that you find during a dive? Definitely not. Empty shells provide safe refuge for a variety of marine organisms, notably hermit crabs.

Some divers are disdainful of the Indonesian or Filipino fisherman who uses cyanide to capture fish for the restaurant or aquarium market. In the world of depleting marine resources it is easy to fall into the scapegoat trap. In fact, we are *all* guilty of creating a huge demand and of consuming products acquired by destructive fishing methods. Aquarium owners should be sure not to purchase fishes captured using cyanide. It is in their financial interest, anyway, since many of those fishes have much reduced life expectancy. Preferably, aquarium owners should demand farmed species.

According to United Nations estimates, on October 12 1999, the world's population reached 6 billion. Our nutritional requirements are staggering. Early man depended on wild megafauna, such as deer and buffalo, to provide him with meat. Today, we realise that breeding animals such as cattle and sheep is the only way to satisfy the rising demand for meat products. The problem with the oceans is that we consume fishes which are high in the food chain and impossible to farm. We cannot replenish depleting stocks of tuna or swordfish. At the same time, fisheries involve substantial bycatch. Here are some disturbing figures: when you purchase a kilo of shrimp, you become an accomplice in the death of about 9 kilos of 'trash fish', such as turtles, seahorses, rays and flounders, that have been dumped back into the ocean as unwanted bycatch. These figures do not include marine life that is considered unworthy of being reported, such as marine plants, sponges, corals, crabs, sea urchins, nudibranchs, snails, sea stars and other bottom dwellers. Trawling for shrimp scrapes the sea floor and creates a moonscape unable to sustain life. In general, marine species declined by 35% between 1970 and 1995, leading to the collapse of several fisheries. About 100 million tonnes of fish are sold each year in fish markets around the globe. WWF estimates the bycatch at 27 million tonnes. How can we remain under the illusion that the marine ecosystem will not collapse due to this continuous destruction?

Aquaculture appears to be the way to satisfy our insatiable appetites. However, keep an eye out for abuses of the concept. 'Tuna farm' is a misleading term, which gives the impression that we can farm tuna and replenish the stocks. However, 'tuna farms' are actually fattening pens that hold wild-caught tuna. Fishing is the opposite of farming. A farmer collects a crop that he has planted. In contrast, a fisherman is a hunter-gatherer who does not replenish his prey.

People order a tuna sandwich or swordfish steak without realising that this is equivalent to living on tiger steak. (The tiger and the tuna are at a similar high level in the food chain.) Yes, fish is good for you. However, you will survive even without eating high-cholesterol shrimp that accounts for about 35% of all bycatch waste. You can make a difference if you stop eating shrimp and predators that are at the top of the marine food chain, such as tuna, swordfish and yahoo. Although mastering buoyancy control to protect the coral reef is of paramount importance, if you then feast at a sushi bar you are not contributing much to the conservation of the marine environment. Reading Sylvia Earle's outstanding book *Sea Change, a Message of the Oceans* made me understand the challenges facing the oceans today. I believe that as a result, I am now an aware consumer of marine products and I hope that you will read it and learn from it too.

The Lembeh Strait Preservation Society

Few divers who come to enjoy the Lembeh Strait are aware that there is a society actively involved in preserving it. The Lembeh Strait Preservation Society was established on April 8 1997, after alarming reports of a high-tech fishing trap operating at the entrance to the strait (on the Tangkoko side). The controversial net complex, armed with an underwater sonar device to attract fishes, had been decimating migratory pelagic populations, including protected species, for over two years. Going against the powerful business concern running the fish trap was not easy. There were times when Captain Billy Matindas, the chairman of the society, feared for his life. One day, he expressed his concerns to his friends.

'Don't worry, Billy,' one of them replied. 'If they kill you, we will name the reserve the Billy Matindas National Marine Park!'

In fact, the society was able to generate enough international pressure to close down the fish trap in April 1998. An investigation showed that the owners had bypassed existing laws. The Indonesian Ministry for the Environment sued them for 180 billion rupiah (about US$20 million). Today, the main objective of the society is to achieve marine park status for the Lembeh Strait, in other words to extend the Tangkoko National Park seaward. Silvester Benny Pratasik volunteered to prepare a scientific report and submit a marine park proposal to the relevant government bodies. I enjoyed diving with Benny and assisted him by supplying the necessary photographs to document his report.

The future of the Lembeh Strait is far from certain. It seems that the society must face several challenges in order to safeguard this highly diverse marine ecosystem. An imminent threat arises from a major gold extraction project. The problem involves the disposal of waste, which will contain cyanide and other highly toxic chemicals. Conservationists believe that, once more, the ocean will become an 'endless' wastebasket. The society fears that this will be the beginning of the end for the Lembeh Strait. Minewatch and other international environmental protection agencies are monitoring this issue.

Further Information

When I began work on this book, I thought it might be a good idea to start a newsletter. I was definitely not prepared for the success of the idea. What I thought would be junk e-mail was viewed as interesting information. Although the plan was that I would live in paradise for five months, away from the 'real' world, my peace of mind became history the moment I surfaced on the electronic air space. I was bombarded by e-mail messages from all over the world. By the time I left KBR, I had written about 100 newsletter pages and answered numerous individual questions about the resort or photography in general.

Some divers had an interesting way of showing their appreciation for my newsletters. On one occasion, I mentioned that my lips were swollen following an encounter with a hydroid or jellyfish. A dear friend, Nafsika, replied, 'Dear Big Lips, I hope you have taken some photos of yourself for posterity, to remind us of your stint as a collagen-enhanced Greek beauty.' Other than that, I think the service was quite popular, since it eventually reached approximately 1,500 addresses.

You are most welcome to check my website www.petrinos.gr and register for the newsletter service. Please do not hesitate to contact me if you have any questions regarding dive travel or equipment. My contact information is as follows:

e-mail: info@petrinos.gr   fax: +30-10-6012-579

Recommended Websites

BBC Natural History Unit Picture Library.
www.bbcwild.com

California Academy of Sciences.
www.calacademy.org

Coral Reef Protection – United States Environmental Protection Agency (EPA), Oceans and Coastal Protection Division (the Related Links section has web addresses of useful sites about marine awareness and conservation).
www.epa.gov/owow/oceans/coral

Global Information System on Fishes.
www.fishbase.org
Information about hotels, diving, adventure and culture in North Sulawesi.
www.north-sulawesi.com

Kungkungan Bay Resort.
www.kungkungan.com

Nudibranchs and other Opisthobranch Molluscs.
www.slugsite.tierranet.com

Ocean Optics – Underwater Photography specialists.
www.oceanoptics.co.uk

Seahorses.
www.seahorse.mcgill.ca

The Undersea and Hyperbaric Medical Society (UHMS).
Information for diving and hyperbaric medicine physiology worldwide.
www.uhms.org

Ultralight Control Systems – modular strobe support arms.
www.ulcs.com

Wildlife Trade.
www.traffic.org

THE CORAL REEF
A COMMUNITY OF CHAOTIC HARMONY

For millennia, we humans have believed that 'we have the right' to claim, conquer, kill and destroy the environment that supports us. We wish to dominate completely. We demand more and more space for ourselves, thus forcing other species into extinction. As a result, on land, wild animals are wise enough to disappear as soon as they sense an approaching *Homo sapiens*, the Number One enemy of all living creatures on the planet.

In contrast, fishes are willing to accept us in their environment, despite our significant criminal record. Diving will give you the opportunity to be among wild creatures for the first time and to observe them. And even though on land I would be afraid to approach an angry dog, underwater I have been in the company of sharks many times without any problem. The more you improve your buoyancy control, the less noisy you will be and fishes will become even more tolerant of your presence.

The underwater world gives you the impression of everlasting peace. Hunters and prey swim side by side. Divers seldom witness a scene of aggression. Attacks usually last a fraction of a second and the victim is swallowed whole before the diver even notices. It was a dusk dive at *Hairball* and there was not much to shoot. Rather than abort the dive, I decided to stay and watch a flying gurnard, *Dactyloptena orientalis*, that was moving along the sandy bottom (see photos p. 46-47). After a while, I noticed the eyes of a painted lizardfish, *Trachinocephalus myops*, sticking out of the sand. Although the gurnard was moving in the direction of the lizardfish, this did not cause me any concern, since it seemed too big for the lizardfish to attack. Imagine my shock when I saw the lizardfish shoot out of the sand with lightning speed and grab the gurnard by the head. I was completely unprepared and it was sheer luck that I was holding the housing with the right lens. The lizardfish had its mouth wide open trying to swallow the poor gurnard, while the latter was hopelessly fighting back by stretching out its pectoral fins. Predators usually swallow their prey head first, otherwise the victim's dorsal fins could stick in their throat, making them choke. I was able to take a few frames before the gurnard disappeared completely.

The small spiny devilfish, *Inimicus didactylus*, shown on page 49 (top), was eating a juvenile fish when my dive guide, Wilson, came upon it. It was having a difficult time swallowing the whole fish and, as a result, Wilson was able to summon me to the scene of the crime. The spiny devilfish is a bottom dweller that will often bury itself in the soft substrate (sand or mud) or sit on the rubble bottom and capture small fish. Let me share an interesting devilfish story with you. One day, an American couple arrived at the resort. Their first dive was scheduled for *Police Pier* at 2 p.m.

'*Police Pier*?' I said to myself. 'What is there left for me to shoot at *Police Pier*? I have done the site inch by inch. I think I'll skip the dive and enjoy a massage.'

The in-house massage at the resort has two advantages: a) it is done by the resort's professional masseuse and sends you to cloud nine, and b) it was the only way I could be tempted to skip a dive and give myself a prolonged surface interval, which is very important when one is doing long, repetitive dives over a period of five months.

My state of nirvana had hardly set in when I heard the divers shouting, 'We've got the devilfish on video!'

This page: Spider crab, Xenocarcinus conicus (1.5cm), on gorgonian with eggs on its abdomen. It also lives on black corals and hydroids. Highly variable in colour, from silver-grey to bright red, it usually has a broad white stripe running down the centre of its carapace.

Opposite: Colubrine sea snake or banded sea krait, Laticauda colubrina (120cm). This species is prized for its smooth leather in the Philippines, where it is heavily collected for use in the large snakeskin industry. Although quite venomous, it is not at all aggressive. Of course divers should not handle or harass a sea snake, but this applies to all creatures.

Previous page: Leather coral, Sinularia sp.

'Big deal,' I thought, 'the place is littered with them.'

However, I did go to watch the video just to kill some time until the night dive. As it turned out, it killed not only time but my mood as well! Imagine the following: a large devilfish is moving along the rubble bottom. Behind it comes an agitated smaller devilfish, with its pectoral fins spread wide open, looking thoroughly menacing. Suddenly, a third devilfish shoots out of the sand (it had lain buried and been impossible to see), moving resolutely towards the bigger of the other two. The large devilfish makes a swift move, grabs the entire head of the intruder in its mouth and starts shaking it. The smaller fish approaches, apparently keen on joining the fight, but, just then, the intruder manages to disengage itself and flee. The other two chase after it.

I was furious with myself and watched that scene on the video at least five times. It just proves that you've got to be out there. 'Tough guys go diving,' as Roger Steene likes to say. The massage may have contributed to my much-needed surface interval, but definitely not to my photography.

The big broadclub cuttlefish, *Sepia latimanus*, opposite resides right in front of the KBR boat pier. She is so well known that she has been given a name – Mary. You are sure to see her by the pier every night. The reason is simple: the strong security lights attract fish and make the pier a prime fishing spot. I always looked for Mary at the end of my night dives just to say hello. As a rule, she seemed oblivious to my presence. I was cautious not to shine a strong light on her face and she sometimes communicated with me by changing colours in a language I could not understand. But, on a particular night, it was obvious that I was not wanted. Mary seemed agitated and unwilling to share her precious meal with me. She swam away.

Cuttlefish and squid have two long tentacles that can be extended like a fishing rod well beyond their remaining eight arms, to capture prey and bring it back to the arms, which hold it securely with their suction cups during ingestion. The tentacles eject and strike the prey with impressive speed. According to R.T. Hanlon & J.B. Messenger (see References, p. 253) in *Sepia officinalis*, the strike time is less than 15 milliseconds (15/1000 second), which is even faster than the strike of the mantis shrimp.

The photographs of the titan triggerfish on page 50 are rather poor one, but I decided to include them because I believe they show an unusual or rarely observed behaviour. I will give you the fun part first, and then the serious bit.

We were diving at *Police Pier*. On my way back to the boat I could not help but notice my spotter, Alki, flirting with a big titan triggerfish, *Balistoides viridescens* (approx. 50cm). The titan was about 20cm from her mask!

'Is she that brave or simply crazy?' I asked myself, and rushed over, thinking that the triggerfish (see photo p. 51), which Alki was admiring, was probably trying to solve a dilemma: which of her ears to bite first... I swam as fast as I could and was expecting the triggerfish to move away at the presence of a charging 'beluga whale', but it did not. End result: there were now two crazy divers sitting 20cm away from the triggerfish and it had *four* ears to choose from. It was hovering in front of our masks and I was convinced I could read its lips saying, 'Make my day...' Not wanting to put its culinary preferences to the test, I decided the time to retreat to a safer distance was long overdue and I motioned to Alki to follow me. As soon as we moved away, the triggerfish started biting a sea cucumber (15-20cm) that was right in front of us. As Alki later explained, she had seen the triggerfish bite the sea cucumber. Apparently, she moved too close and the triggerfish interrupted its meal but decided to stay and guard its prey. Personally, I was too scared to take notice of the sea cucumber until we stepped back.

Previous page: Painted lizardfish or snakefish, Trachinocephalus myops (33cm), eating a flying gurnard, Dactyloptena orientalis (38cm).

Opposite top: Spiny devilfish, Inimicus didactylus (18cm), eating a juvenile fish.

Opposite middle: Mary, the broadclub cuttlefish, Sepia latimanus (50cm), that used to hunt at night by the lights of the KBR pier. The lights attracted the fish and Mary was able to pick up an easy supper. On another occasion, I was videotaping a big Sepia latimanus during a night dive at Jiko Yansi. The cuttlefish was using the chromatophores under its skin to make all sorts of displays and colour changes. Seeing that I was a persistent 'predator', it resorted to a unique and impressive cephalopod display: the passing cloud. The skin of the cuttlefish resembled a flashing neon sign as dark waves swept across its body. By that time, despite our linguistic differences, the message had come across: I was not wanted. But, with the greed characteristic of underwater photographers, I pursued the cuttlefish as it swam over the reef. Suddenly, it stopped, turned to face me, spat out the leftovers of an eel and disappeared! Seeing that it could not escape from the predator, it had decided as a last resort to distract him by offering him its dinner. I was so startled that I did not see where the cuttlefish went. The diversion had enabled it to vanish. This complex behaviour reflects the fact that cephalopods are highly intelligent. The bottom line is, of course, that I had disturbed the cuttlefish and made it waste a precious meal.

Opposite bottom: Swimming crab, Charybdis sp., eating a starfish.

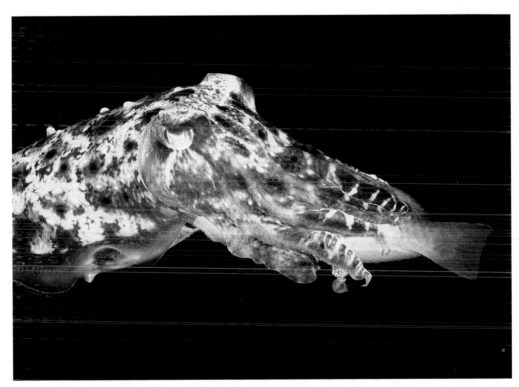

The titan triggerfish is famous for its strong teeth and stealth. Even the sea urchin's spines are not a deterrent for the mighty titan. If a sea urchin makes the mistake of going for a walk in the morning, it may become an easy meal for the titan, which turns it around, bites the underside (which has shorter spines) and consumes the flesh. I have also seen a titan at *Goby-A-Crab* break some hard coral with amazing determination, to reach a crab that was trying to hide. It broke the crab's carapace as though it were made of rice paper.

So, the titan feeds on echinoids and crustaceans. But what about sea cucumbers? Was this a major discovery? Was I going to be famous? I contacted the highly regarded ichthyologist Dr John E. Randall. He replied, 'Although I have never examined a *Balistoides viridescens* for stomach contents, I have no knowledge that it feeds on sea cucumbers. But surely I would have seen or heard that sea cucumbers are a normal item of diet for the titan, if it is so. Maybe it is a food item that is eaten when the fish is very hungry and can't find something else.'

Holothurians (sea cucumbers) can be seen sitting exposed on the reef in broad daylight. If they were part of the Titan's normal diet and their only defence was their tough skin – not a deterrent for the Titan's jaws of steel – I think that they would soon become extinct, unless they decided to become nocturnal. Obviously, since they are plentiful and available, they must have some sort of defence to avoid predation. Many holothurians are toxic. The toxin is stored in white spaghetti-like sticky structures known as Cuvierian tubules, which are attached to the animal's respiratory trees. To discourage potential predators, the sea cucumber must inform them of its toxicity and the possibility of entanglement in its sticky threads. Some species expel the Cuvierian tubules while others eviscerate, ejecting the entire digestive system, including the respiratory trees and gonads. All lost body parts are regenerated.

If the species in the photograph, cf. *Holothuria impatiens*, were toxic, the sea cucumber should have reacted immediately by eviscerating at the titan's first bite. However, nothing of the sort happened and the titan, not wanting to share its prey with us, took it under a ledge and consumed it in peace. I have rarely noticed a sea cucumber of this species in the Lembeh Strait; so perhaps it suffers from predation pressure after all.

During a rather uninteresting dive at *Aer Parang*, my buddy decided to ascend to the boat and enjoy the sunshine. As I had plenty of air left, it would have been a breach of my principles to abort the dive, despite the temptation of the exotic fruits waiting on board. Iwan, a senior KBR dive guide, started checking his favourite spots again, one by one. No luck; it was not my day. I would have to come back again, and with this thought, I decided to ascend. Suddenly, Iwan pulled me by my BCD and started pointing frantically at the bottom. I took a look, but there was nothing, and I continued my ascent towards the fruit basket on board our boat. But Iwan seemed determined. He was pointing desperately to an area right under my feet. He was so excited, his eyes were about to pop out of the mask. 'You should check your blood pressure, young man,' I thought to myself.

I stopped my ascent, looked right under my feet, but still there was nothing. Then Iwan pulled me to the side. Yes! Now that I was at a different angle, I could see it. An unusual octopus! Fortunately, we were in midwater and all the commotion had not startled it. With swift movements, the wonderpus engulfed a stone, creating a fishing net with the web between its arms and reached under the rock with the tips of its tentacles to look for crab or shrimp (see photo p. 53).

This page: Titan triggerfish, Balistoides viridescens (75cm), eating a sea cucumber, cf. Holothuria impatiens (40cm).

Opposite: The titan was hovering in front of our masks and I was convinced I could read its lips saying, 'Make my day...'

This page: Wonderpus, Octopus sp. (25cm), using the web between its legs to create a fishing net.

Opposite: Yellowmargin triggerfish, Pseudobalistes flavimarginatus (60cm), feeding. The triggerfish stirs up the sand by blasting a stream of water. In this way it exposes the snails that are burried under the sand. Their shells provide no protection to the mollusk when confronted with the powerful teeth of the triggerfish.

There is nothing the neon fusilier, *Pterocaesio tile*, in the photograph opposite (top) can do to get rid of the parasitic isopod (*Cymothoidae*), a louse-like crustacean that hooks itself onto the fish's skin, using its seven pairs of hooklike legs. It then bites its victim like a vampire, living off the blood and bodily fluids. This does not lead to slow death for the fish, as one might expect. Usually, the host has minor symptoms, such as scale erosion and skin discolouration. In extreme cases, this long-term relationship may lead to some bone deformities.

Being crustaceans, isopods face an interesting dilemma when they must moult their exoskeleton. If they were to shed their entire shell at one time, like other crustaceans, they would have to unhook themselves from their victim. The result would be death, since isopods lose their ability to swim freely once they settle on a fish. Therefore, they undergo a two-stage moulting process. First, they moult the front half of their bodies and, once the new exoskeleton is hard enough, they proceed to moult the other half.

Isopods are protandrous (Gr: first male) hermaphrodites. The juveniles start their life as free-swimming males. If they find a female when they settle on a fish, they mate. The female may incubate over 100 isopods inside her ventral pouch. Once the offspring hatch, the female dies and the male changes sex and waits for another male to settle, so as to repeat the process. On the other hand, if the male does not find a female upon settling on his host, he prematurely changes into a female by accelerating his growth rate. In general, marine isopods parasitise a wide range of animals: fishes, cephalopods, crustaceans and even other isopods.

The male Coleman shrimp, *Periclimenes colemani*, in the photograph on this page, is under attack from a pair of parasitic isopods. These are branchial parasites, living in pairs on the gills of shrimp. The female is the large animal that fills the shrimp's gill. As a result, that side of the shrimp's carapace is swollen, enabling us to detect the presence of the isopods. The male is a tiny creature whose sole purpose is to fertilise the many eggs produced by the female. Sometimes, the shrimp may have both sides of its carapace swollen, indicating the presence of two pairs of isopods.

What does a marine snail eat? Snails are voracious predators and eat a wide range of things, including other snails. The muricid snail *Drupella cornus* eats corals, cone snails prey on fishes and the giant triton, *Charonia tritonis*, preys on the crown-of-thorns starfish, *Acanthaster planci*. In the photo opposite (bottom), the snail is preying on a corallimorpharian, *Pseudocorynactis* sp. The latter are considered intermediate between hard corals and sea anemones. Their anatomy has the characteristics of hard corals, but lacks the hard skeleton, as do anemones. The picture was taken during daytime at *Police Pier*. The snail ate the corallimorpharian in approximately half an hour.

Mandarin fish, *Synchiropus splendidus*, occupy a small territory on coastal reefs and lagoon bommies. Unfortunately, their spectacular colours make them a highly prized possession for the aquarium trade. The major exporter is the Philippines, where they are fished primarily with cyanide. The fact that mandarin fish claim a small territory on the reef makes them suitable for the tight living quarters of an aquarium. Their tolerance of the unnatural aquarium environment is such that they can even survive in pairs. Pseudo-spawning and even true spawning have been observed in aquaria. In the restricted confines of an aquarium male mandarin fish will sometimes engage in a fight to protect their territory.

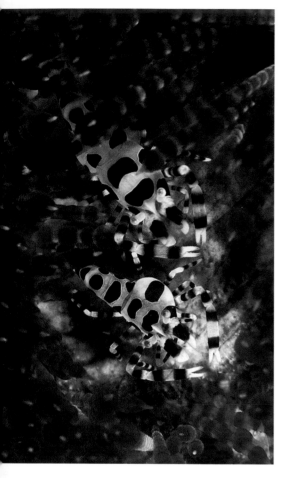

This page: The smaller Coleman shrimp, Periclimenes colemani (2cm), is the male and the larger the female. The left-hand side of the male's carapace is swollen, indicating the presence of parasitic isopods.

Opposite top: Isopod parasite, Cymothoidae, attacking a neon fusilier, Pterocaesio tile (25cm). This picture was taken during a night dive, when the lower half of the neon fusilier's body turns from silver to bright red.

Opposite middle: Slipper lobster, Thenus sp. (20cm), examining a shell. Crabs are known scavengers and are often seen eating leftovers. Everything is examined meticulously for that precious morsel of food that may have been left over. Unfortunately for this slipper lobster, the shell was empty. But persistence will eventually pay off.

Opposite bottom: Cowrie, Cypraea sp., eating a corallimorpharian, Pseudocorynactis sp.

This page: Two different Stonogobiops species sharing a burrow. The one with the long first dorsal fin is Stonogobiops nematodes (6cm) and the other is Stonogobiops xanthorhinica (5.5cm).

Opposite top: Polycerid nudibranch, Nembrotha rutilans (5cm), feeding on sea squirts.

Opposite middle: The carcass of a lobster becomes a gourmet meal for a sea urchin.

Opposite bottom: Spearer mantis shrimp, Lysiosquilloides sp. (25cm). The eyes move independently, looking in two directions.

Previous page: Male mandarin fish, Synchiropus splendidus (6cm), engaged in a fight.

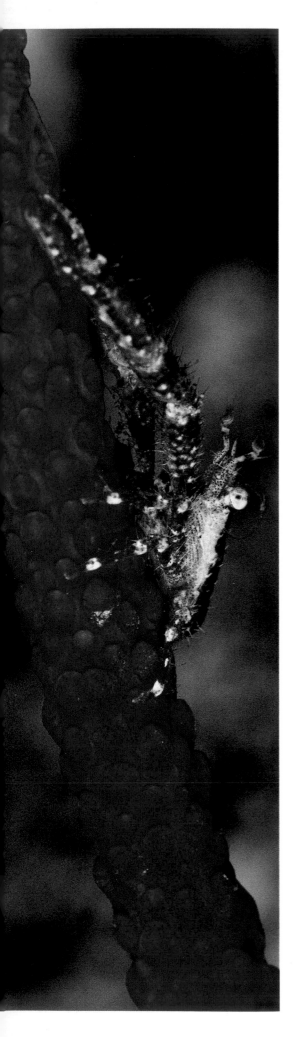

Lettus Surpriz U is the dive site that has become famous for its prolific numbers of mandarin fish. We went to a very small area of coral rubble for a dusk dive. As night fell, tiny 'rainbows' started emerging from the chaotic surroundings to feed onminuscule crustacea and other small benthic organisms. I could not believe my eyes – there were literally hundreds of mandarin fish. I had seen one once in Fiji, but only for a few seconds. At the time I was satisfied, since for most divers seeing a mandarin fish is like a dream come true.

In this instance, I went back to KBR puzzled by the sheer abundance of this species in a relatively small area. It could be that their natural predators were absent from that particular location or that there was plenty of food to be had. Or both. I read again and again everything on mandarin fish that I could find in the KBR library. Reading about the territorial fights in aquaria spurred my imagination. Could the relatively limited space and the sheer numbers of mandarin fish make the conditions analogous to those of an aquarium? Perhaps that could lead to two males fighting over a territory. Obsessed with the idea, I visited the area a few more times, until one night, we saw two males fighting. Each was in full display, trying to intimidate his opponent. In a split second, one attacked, biting the other's neck! The two fish swirled in this deadly embrace for a few seconds, until the loser fled away to seek another territory. Photographs exist of mandarin fish spawning, and that type of shot is usually the best one can ever hope for. However, the photograph on pages 56-57 is probably the first recorded scene of mandarin fish fighting in their natural habitat. It is one of my most prized pictures. The technical difficulties were substantial, given the small size of the fish (approx. 5cm) and the fact that the fighting took place under a broken piece of hard coral.

On page 59 we have something rather unusual: two *Stonogobiops* species sharing the same burrow. The one with the long first dorsal fin is *Stonogobiops nematodes* and the other is *Stonogobiops xanthorhinica*. I saw them at a depth of 20m at the rubble slope of *Nudi Falls* but was unable to take a picture due to the strong current. I marked the spot and returned at slack tide, but by then the gobies were hidden inside the burrow. Obviously, there was no reason for them to expose themselves to the dangers of the open ocean, since there was no current to bring them lunch. I returned when there was current, and found both fishes outside the burrow, feeding on the nutrients brought to them by the current.

The rubble slope of *Nudi Falls* leads to the Lembeh channel and, as a result, it is particularly exposed to strong currents, even when there is no current near the shore. The fishes were skittish and disappeared into their burrow at the slightest sign of a threat. It was then some time before they re-emerged which, given the depth, drove my Aladin dive computer crazy. The only way I could take a picture was by using my 200mm lens.

On my third attempt to photograph the fish, I noticed a second and smaller *Stonogobiops xanthorhinica* entering the burrow and trying to evict the *Stonogobiops nematodes*, which was apparently the intruder. Despite several tries, the small fish was driven away by the larger *nematodes* species. However, it seems that, eventually, it succeeded, since on several subsequent dives I saw only the pair of *Stonogobiops xanthorhinica* in that burrow. Incidentally, there were also two red snapping shrimp, *Alpheus randalli*, sharing the same burrow with the gobies.

This page top: Smasher mantis shrimp, Oratosquilla oratoria (15cm).

This page bottom: Smasher mantis shrimp, Odontodactylus scyallarus (18cm). With its impressive colours, this species is one of the best examples of aposematic coloration, i.e. vivid colours used to signal to potential predators 'I am dangerous!'

Opposite: Squat lobster on sea whip, Junceella sp.

Overleaf: Compound eyes of the smasher mantis shrimp, Odontodactylus scyallarus (18cm).

If you think that the titan triggerfish has a fiery temperament, wait till you meet the mantis shrimp, a fearsome and violent carnivorous predator. This lobster-like crustacean separated from the crustacean evolutionary line about 400 million years ago, forming a distinct subclass called Stomatopoda. Today, there are about 350 mantis shrimp species.

Their bodies are large and may reach 35cm. The feature that distinguishes them from other crustaceans is the fact that they are not decapods, but have only eight pairs of thoracic legs. The second pair comprises two large, very powerful and specialised hunting weapons, called raptorial legs. Some are designed to work like spears and others like smashing clubs.

The animal's lifestyle varies according to its weaponry and hunting method. Spearers stay in their burrow and ambush soft-bodied prey, such as fish or shrimp, spearing the victim and consuming it inside the burrow. The strike speed is impressive: up to 10m per second! Smashers hide inside reef crevices. They are the mantis shrimps that you see foraging around the reef, looking for hard-shelled prey, such as crabs and snails, and smashing the shells with their club-like raptorial legs to gain access to the flesh.

Having sophisticated weaponry is worthless unless you have the radar equipment to detect the target and direct your weapon with precision. The compound eyes of the mantis (see photo p. 62-63) could not be better suited for target acquisition. To give you a rough idea, the human eye has one lens, whereas the compound eye is the sum of several thousand units called ommatidia (Gr: little eyes). Each ommatidium has one fixed-focus lens with a large depth of field. Its shape is convex; therefore, lens orientation differs slightly from one ommatidium to the other. The result is that you cannot surprise a mantis shrimp or any other crustacean, because they have a very wide field of vision. On top of that, the mantis shrimp's eyes are on movable stalks. Like lobsters, they cannot turn their head because of their body structure. However, they can independently rotate each eyeball through 360 degrees!

Have you ever wondered how a mantis shrimp perceives you? Certainly not like thousands of identical little divers, the way killer bees view people in science-fiction movies. Their vision is not kaleidoscopic. Each fixed-focus lens sees a fraction of the picture and their sum makes up a single image, like a finished puzzle. Without fixed-focal lenses, the compound image would give the mantis quite a headache. Although the compound eye produces a single picture, the image is quite coarse-grained because of lens quality. This is simple to understand if you are a photographer. Good optics in a camera lens are directly associated with large size and vice versa. To get the same wide field of view with a single lens (high-quality vision) the mantis shrimp's eyes would have to be huge, and I doubt whether it would be able to carry them. In optics, one has to choose. For the mantis, a wide field of vision is the top priority. With compound eyes, crustaceans sacrifice optics quality to get the widest possible field of vision with a compact design.

This page: Smasher mantis shrimp, Odontodactylus latirostris (8cm).

Opposite: Mushroom coral detail.

Overleaf: This decorator crab, Hoplophrys oatesii (1.5cm), lives with Dendronephthya soft corals and mimics the colour of its coral host.

SURVIVAL RECIPES

Underwater, you may not see bloody scenes, like lions feeding on their kill, or hear the sound of bones being crushed as hyenas bite into their victim's carcass, or smell death as you do on the African savannah, but, if you learn to observe carefully, you will notice that it is a violent world, even down here. It is interesting to observe the different means each creature uses to avoid being eaten. Some seek protection from a 'godfather', others build a burrow, while still others bury themselves under the sand, use camouflage colours or mimic other life forms. Some creatures resort to chemical warfare to protect themselves. When it senses danger, the nudibranch *Glossodoris hikuerensis* secretes a toxic slime to protect itself (see photo p. 176).

Divers are impressed by the size of barrel sponges and usually pass them by, as if they were dead rock. However, these sponges are a safe haven for the otherwise homeless. Their cavities are excellent 'trenches' for a host of creatures such as crabs, fish or shrimp. Their labyrinthine structure provides escape routes and alternative hideouts. If you examine one of the many barrel sponges, *Xestospongia* sp., in the Lembeh Strait closely, you will be amazed at the profusion of life (see photo p. 71).

Crustaceans are a delicacy for a variety of fish and an important part of the food chain since a wide range of animals depend on them for their survival. Given the high predation pressure, crustaceans have adopted secretive lifestyles and cryptic behaviour. They spend their days hiding in burrows or reef crevices. As a result, divers see only a small fraction of the more than 45,000 species and may fail to realise the diversity of this group. At dusk, most bottom-foraging predators retreat to a safe place to spend the night. This makes life less dangerous for the crustaceans, who take the opportunity to emerge from their hideouts to feed. Of course they have to be vigilant for nocturnally active predators such as cuttlefishes, octopuses and lionfishes.

The bottom line of this discussion is that if you want to see crabs or shrimps you must show some strength of character and skip those nice cold beers on the KBR restaurant verandah, while admiring the sunset over Lembeh Strait. Not being much of a drinker, I must say I enjoyed my KBR night dives tremendously. Crustaceans are very conscious of the risks they face, and this makes them extremely cautious and skittish. 'Better safe than sorry' is the principle that governs their lifestyle. When I started night diving, I bought the most powerful dive light that I could afford. This was a very good light indeed. It made the salesman richer and had a therapeutic effect on my primordial fears about the dark. But it ruined my night dives by scaring all the creatures away with its strong beam. You will have limited chances of observing crustaceans at night, unless you use a relatively weak dive light that does not frighten the animals. Also be particularly careful of 'resort lionfishes'. It takes very little time for lionfishes that are resident in house reefs to realise that divers are associated with food. Night divers will frighten a shrimp with their powerful dive lights and expose it to a lionfish, which is presented with an easy meal. Eventually, the lionfish will come closer to the diver, trying to get a better look. The reason I can describe the application of Pavlov's theory to fish so accurately is that I was once stung by such a resort lionfish.

When crabs have to make a crossing in the open, it is safer to use camouflage, much as soldiers do when crossing an exposed area. Sponge crabs, *Dromiidae*, use their rear legs to carry a piece of sponge over their backs. The sponge continues to grow and eventually covers the carapace. The first time you see a sponge start to walk, it may be a good reminder that you should never drink alcohol before a dive.

This page: The squat lobster, Allogalathea elegans (2cm), is usually found living in association with crinoids. However, this individual was photographed on a sponge, during a night dive, with no crinoid in the vicinity. It will probably hop on to a crinoid when the opportunity arises.

Opposite: Moray eel sneaking out from a palm tree branch that fell in the water with the monsoons.

It was one of my countless night dives in front of the resort's pier and I was moving around, checking to see what my 'regulars' were doing. There was a full moon and it was simply fun to be underwater. At the end of my 98-minute dive, I witnessed an incredible scene, right under the pier. I found two huge sponge crabs, *Dromia dormia*, engaged in a fight. One was carrying a yellow sponge and the other a purple one. With their chelipeds extended, they looked like two mighty warriors. What a shot! The crabs were so big that I needed a wide-angle lens. However, I did enjoy the spectacle tremendously. One of them had only one claw and it was, eventually, the loser who had to flee.

Hermit crabs (see photo p. 78) are a standard feature of KBR night dives. The first pair of their walking legs is equipped with claws, whereas the fourth or fifth pair is reduced in size. Like all Anomuran crabs, they have an evident tail section. Their large, soft abdomen is not protected by a carapace, making them an easy and tasty meal for a host of predators. To protect themselves, they hide inside empty snail shells. When they outgrow this temporary home, they simply have to switch to a bigger shell that will accommodate them better. Divers who collect empty shells reduce the housing options for hermit crabs.

The largest hermit crab is the coconut crab, *Birgus latro*, which lives on land. However, as with all land crabs, its eggs hatch in the sea. After the larval development is complete, small juveniles seek a shell to protect themselves, like all hermit crabs. They later abandon their shell and return to land, where they live near the shore without using a shell.

Dardanus pedunculatus is the most common species of hermit crab in the Lembeh Strait. Once the crab has found a suitable shell, it moves into its new apartment and then places small sea anemones on the shell. This is a mutually beneficial relationship. The crab gains camouflage and protection. The sea anemone, a sedentary animal, obtains free transportation to different feeding locations. In addition, the crab protects the anemones from predation by polychaete worms. Such a mutually beneficial relationship between two different species living in association is called mutualism.

Decorator crabs, *Majidae*, are the plastic surgeons of the coral reef (see photos p. 75, 77). They can alter their appearance by prosthetic surgery. Sponges, sea anemones, algae, hydroids and tunicates are carefully selected and implanted all over their body and legs. The crab secures the various camouflage items using the patches of small hair-like hooks (setae) that stick out of its exoskeleton. As a result, decorator crabs blend with the coral reef and are invisible unless they decide to move.

In contrast with hermit crabs, decorator crabs do not have an obvious tail section. They belong to the true crabs or Brachyurans (Gr: short-tailed) whose shell covers their entire body. This better armour has its advantages and disadvantages. Their bodies are better protected than the hermit crab's, but as they grow bigger they have to shed their hide during the moulting process. The crab absorbs calcium salts from the old exoskeleton (cuticle) to help the development of the new shell. Eventually, it sheds the old shell and appears in its new clothes that are made to fit. Sometimes, crustaceans will eat part of the old exoskeleton as a calcium supplement to help harden the new cuticle. As the new shell is relatively soft, this is the time when true crabs are particularly vulnerable. Until their new armour strengthens, they have to be even more wary of potential predators.

Opposite: The squat lobster, Lauriea siagiani (1.5cm), lives on barrel sponges. With the bristles (setae) that cover its body, it is able to sense changes in water movement and disappear into a sponge cavity at the approach of a predator, whether it is a fish or a photographer. The name 'lobster' derives from the fact that the arms that bear the claws, called chelipeds, are long. The one pictured overleaf has lost a cheliped. Will it be crippled for life? Of course not! If you look carefully, you will notice that it has already started to regenerate the missing limb.

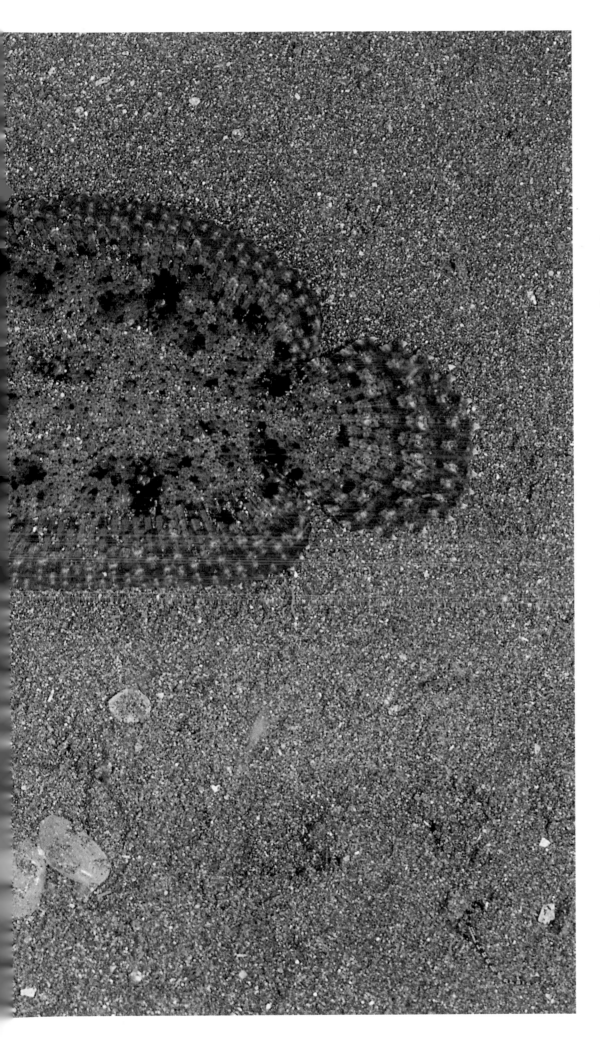

This page: Like many bottom dwelling species, flounders rely on camouflage to avoid detection by potential predators or prey. They are able to fine tune their coloration to blend perfectly with the substrate. The cockatoo righteye flounder, Samaris Cristatus (22cm), has a fall back plan if its primary defense - camouflage - fails. Its first 12-15 (rarely 10-11) anterior dorsal-fin rays are white and greatly elongated. They are normally tucked under the whitish blind side of its body. If a potential predator is not fooled by the excellent camouflage and manages to detect the flounder, the latter extends the white rays like a fan in order to frighten off the predator. In fact, although I had done my homework beforehand, when the flounder extended its elongated dorsal-fin rays, I was foolishly taken off guard. Because the founder matches perfectly the monochromatic sandy background, once it extends the white rays, the colour contrast is such that it creates an effect similar to the white flash of a strobe firing at you. Other than trying to give its potential predator a heart attack, this flounder is harmless. It has a wide distribution range in the Indo-West Pacific and, although this picture was taken at Secret Bay in Bali, I decided to include it in the book because the Lomboh Strait has several sites with sandy substrates, which are ideal habitats for this species found in Indonesian waters.

Page 74 top: Sponge crab, Cryptodromia sp.

Page 74 bottom: Sponge crab, Dromia dormia (20cm).

Page 75: Decorator crab, Cyclocoeloma tuberculata (5cm). The carapace of this crab is covered with corallimorpharians, Discosoma sp. After the moulting process, the crab will have to acquire new live camouflage. He can either transfer the corallimorpharians from one shell to the other or simply look for a new camouflage combination.

73

In general, crabs are the taxi drivers of the reef. They seem to sign contracts with sedentary or slow-moving animals and offer free transportation to different restaurants in exchange for camouflage and protection. A sea urchin is obviously an excellent choice. The crab *Dorippe frascone* (see photo p. 90) digs under the sea urchin and uses its third and fourth pairs of legs to hold the urchin on its back. It can then walk around in almost absolute safety. However, to be on the safe side, when it senses danger it quickly burrows under the sand, leaving the sea urchin on top. When all is clear, it picks up the sea urchin again and off they go. The first time you see urchins moving along with lightning speed you may think you are in Alice's Wonderland, but then, don't forget, you are in Lembeh Strait, where everything is possible.

Some predators, such as triggerfishes, groupers and puffers, show little respect for the sea urchin's formidable spines. To avoid becoming a gourmet meal, sea urchins spend the day wedged in crevices or under rocks. They are nocturnal. Many species feed on algae; others primarily on bryozoans, ascidians and sponges. When they find themselves exposed in the open during daylight, they form aggregations to defend themselves against predators (see photo p. 88-89). At *Hairball*, you will find clusters of *Astropyga radiata* during the day. You will be surprised at how fast these big urchins can move, while maintaining their protective formation. If they were to rely on their tube feet alone, they would be as slow as their starfish relatives. However, the spines on the underside provide leverage that has a dramatic effect on speed. In the exposed sandy landscape of *Hairball*, these sea urchin aggregations are like safe houses for crustaceans and fishes who find refuge among the forests of sharp spines.

The juvenile red emperor, *Lutjanus sebae* (see photo p. 192-193), uses the sea urchin *Astropyga radiata* as a refuge until it comes of age, at which time it leaves its host and moves into deep water. As the fish approaches adulthood, the broad black bands turn into brown. Eventually, the bands disappear, and the adults, which reach 60cm, have a deep red colour. Cardinalfishes, *Apogon* sp., also use this urchin for shelter. The symbiont (juvenile red emperor) does not pay a 'fee' to its host (sea urchin) for services rendered. A relationship between two different species living in association, whereby one benefits and the other neither gains nor loses, is called commensalism. In cases where one species lives at the expense of its host, we have parasitism.

This page: A shrimp, Rhynchocinetes sp. (4-5cm), hiding in the cavity of a barrel sponge, Xestospongia sp. Notice that it has one antenna pointing forward and the other pointing backwards, so as to be able to sense a predator approaching from either direction.

Opposite: Decorator crab, Cyclocoeloma tuberculata (5cm) covered with corallimorpharians, Discosoma sp.

Shell-breaking hermit crab, Dardanus megistos (15cm). As well as being a scavenger, this large hermit crab is able to break a mollusc's shell and feed on the animal.

Sponge crab, Lauridromia dehaani (12cm).

The toxic sea urchin or fire urchin, *Asthenosoma varium*, is among the biggest sea urchins and one of the most venomous echinoids. The venom is stored in sacs located at the tips of its sharp spines. When a spine penetrates the skin, the venom enters the wound, causing excruciating pain. If you happen to get stung by several spines, multiply the pain factor accordingly. The victim experiences intense radiating pain and, depending on the extent of the wound, possibly faintness, numbness, muscular paralysis, loss of speech, respiratory distress and even death. The intense pain and muscular paralysis may last for several hours. Rescuers may have to conduct artificial respiration. The victim may have a strong allergic reaction, in which case adrenalin and antihistamines may be required. Medical attention is strongly advised. Surgical intervention may be required to remove the spines, particularly if they have penetrated a bone joint. Otherwise, there is the danger of severe chronic inflammatory reaction. In general, divers should be particularly cautious with sea urchins, especially on night dives, when these creatures come out to feed. Their needlelike spines and pedicellariae represent a real threat, despite the fact that they do not feature in movies like *Jaws*. There are no specific antivenins available for sea urchin stings.

With such impressive weaponry, it is not surprising that the toxic sea urchin attracts commensal species, such as the zebra crab, *Zebrida adamsii*, and the shrimps *Allopontonia iaini* and *Periclimenes colemani*. The latter is found exclusively in association with this species of urchin.

The shrimps seem perfectly happy living in a poisonous forest. Their first task is to create some open space by cutting off a few tube feet and spines. They then spend their lives occupying this patch. However, if they feel like examining the limits of their world, they can move among the venomous spines and pedicellariae without being harmed. Despite its impressive armour, even the toxic sea urchin is not immune to a parasitic attack by the snail *Leutzenia asthenosomae*. In the Lembeh Strait, toxic sea urchins are sure to be found on the walls of *Jiko Yansi*.

Although crustaceans have to lead secretive lives in order to survive, cleaner shrimps need to advertise their presence in broad daylight, by wearing vivid colours and waving their long antennae to attract crustacean predators and obtain their food by cleaning them. These reef doctors set up permanent cleaning stations and are patronised by a wide clientele, such as groupers and moray eels. During office hours, patients assume a hovering position near the station. The shrimp jumps fearlessly onto the fish and starts a routine inspection. It checks the mouth and gills and removes parasites, supplementing its diet from the mucous coat of the fish. The banded coral shrimp, Stenopus hispidus (5cm), is a common cleaner shrimp. Notice the tiny fish next to the left cheliped.

Opposite: A spearer mantis shrimp, Lysiosquillina sp. (25cm), a ferocious predator, is rarely, if ever, seen outside its burrow. Since this patient is unwilling to visit a cleaning station, Stenopus tenuirostris (2cm) is obliged to make a house call and offer its cleaning services.

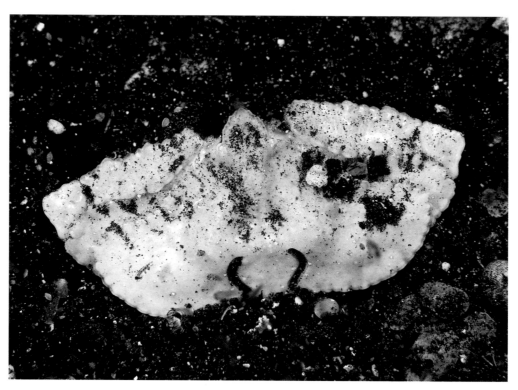

This page: Shrimp, Periclimenes sp.

Opposite top: Tozeuma shrimp, Tozeuma sp.

Opposite middle: Interesting-looking crab, Cryptopodia sp. (4cm).

Opposite bottom: Many shrimps do not have the privileges associated with commensal relationships. Like crabs, they bury themselves in the sand when threatened. This shrimp, Sicyonia sp., photographed during a night dive at Hairball, disappeared under the sand as soon as my strobes fired.

Previous page: This is a typical muck dive site. There is nowhere to hide for these sea urchins, Astropyga radiata (20cm). As a result, they form an aggregation to defend themselves against diurnal predators. The forests of their spines become a safeheaven for fishes and crustaceans, such as the zebra crab on the opposite page.

This page: Crabs take maximum advantage of sea urchins in order to protect themselves. In this picture, a dorippid crab, Dorippe frascone (4cm), is carrying a sea urchin, Astropyga radiata, with its third and fourth pairs of legs.

Opposite: The zebra crab, Zebrida adamsii (1.5cm), lives in association with several sea urchin species. Here it is seen on an Astropyga radiata.

Holothurians or sea cucumbers are host to several commensal species of small crustaceans. Sea cucumbers are the vacuum cleaners of the ocean floor. They may seem lazy, but in fact they filter a huge amount of sediment per day. The nutrients are absorbed as the sand moves through their tube-like digestive tract. The anus excretes the processed sand, leaving a characteristic trail on the bottom. The sea cucumber has plenty of food and can spare some for the tiny guests who are willing to venture inside its anus and enter its digestive tract. In addition, it offers safe accommodation and free travel. The harlequin crab retreats inside the sea cucumber's anus when it feels threatened. The pearlfish, *Carapus* sp., also views the anus as a perfect burrow.

Unfortunately, sea cucumbers are victims of indiscriminate and intensive harvesting. Commercially, they are referred to as trepang or bêche-de-mer. The live animals are gutted, boiled, smoked and then dried. It seems unjustifiable that they should have to suffer a torturous death to serve our culinary eccentricities. Dried sea cucumbers are used as a base for soups in Asian cuisine. When boiled, the animal's thick, leathery skin becomes a tasteless, gelatinous substance. In Traditional Chinese Medicine, sea cucumbers have various dubious therapeutic properties, including the ability to enhance sexual potency. In my opinion, people should try Viagra and leave the poor creatures alone. Note that even in this case, there is significant bycatch involved, namely the commensal animals living on the holothurians that are harvested.

The demand for sea cucumbers induced several South Pacific communities to shift to large-scale exploitation. In 1992 exports from the Solomon Islands and Fiji reached 1,100 tonnes and were worth US$7 million! It should be stressed that the weight of the exported product is not indicative of the number of animals harvested. During processing, the length and weight of animals is reduced to about 10% of their original size – in this case about 11,000 tonnes. Some communities have already depleted the sea cucumber fishery in the vicinity of their village.

According to TRAFFIC International – the wildlife trade monitoring programme of the World Wide Fund for Nature (WWF) and the World Conservation Union (IUCN) – out of all South Pacific nations, only Fiji and Vanuatu have established controls (over weight and size) in the sea cucumber fishery. In the Solomon Islands, the fisheries department is examining whether it is possible to restock the depleted reefs with aquaculture-produced juveniles.

The small yellow *Colochirus robustus* (6cm) on page 94 is not harvested. This sea cucumber is characterised by branched feeding tentacles and forms aggregations in areas that are exposed to strong currents, such as the walls at *Jiko Yansi*. Each individual uses its five branched tentacles to trap the plankton brought to it by the current. Although it has tube feet, once it chooses an appropriate feeding spot it rarely changes position. Divers sometimes confuse this holothurian with a nudibranch.

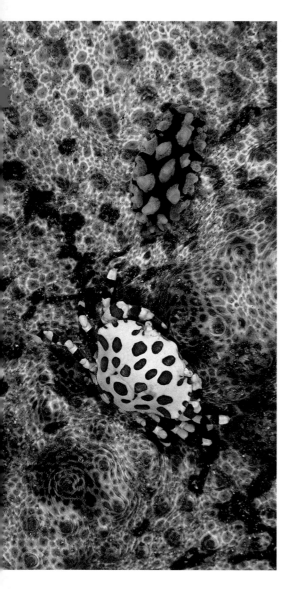

This page: Harlequin crab, Lissocarcinus orbicularis (4cm), and nudibranch, Fryeria menindie (5.4cm), on sea cucumber. The nudibranch is not associated with the sea cucumber. It is just crossing the 'mountain' it encountered along its way.

Opposite: Imperial shrimp, Periclimenes imperator (2cm), and tiny harlequin crab, Lissocarcinus orbicularis (4cm), on sea cucumber, Bohadschia argus (40cm).

Page 94: Holothurian, Colochirus robustus (6cm).

Page 95: Pink anemonefish, Amphiprion perideraion (10cm), and host anemone, Heteractis magnifica.

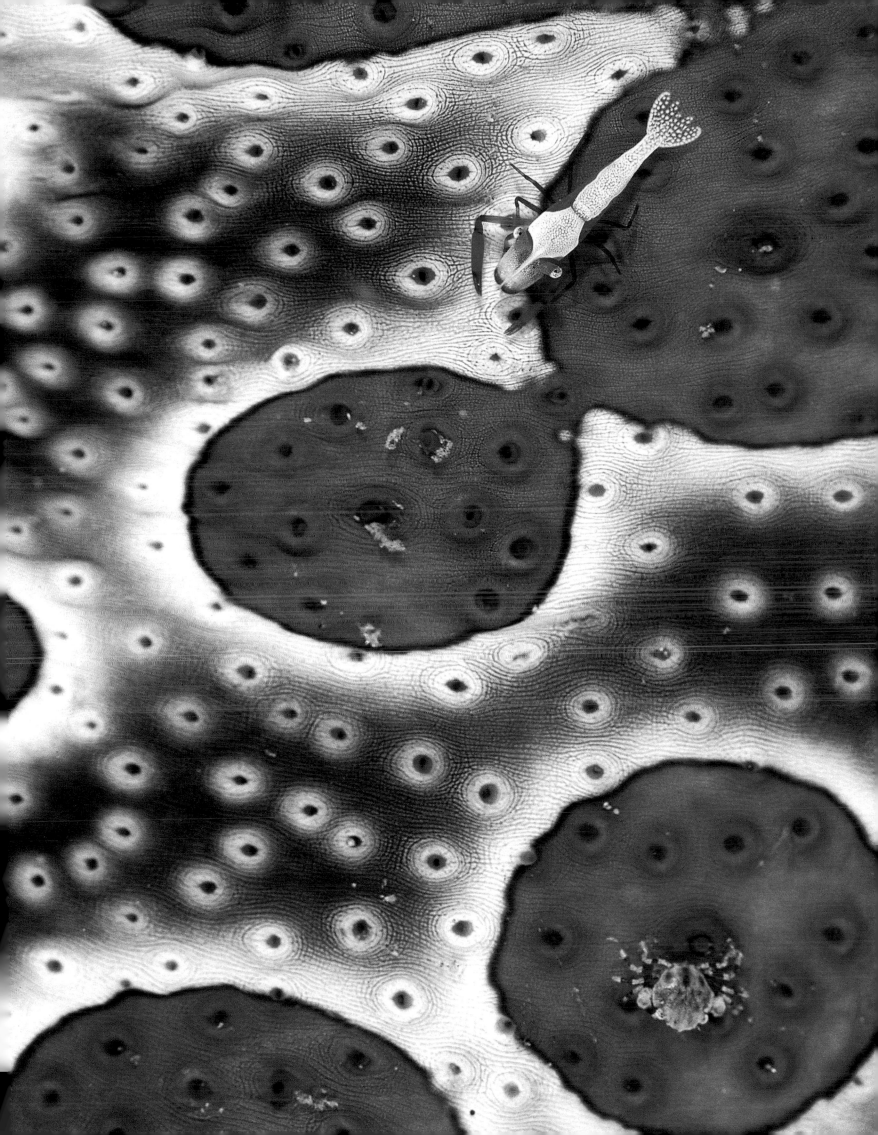

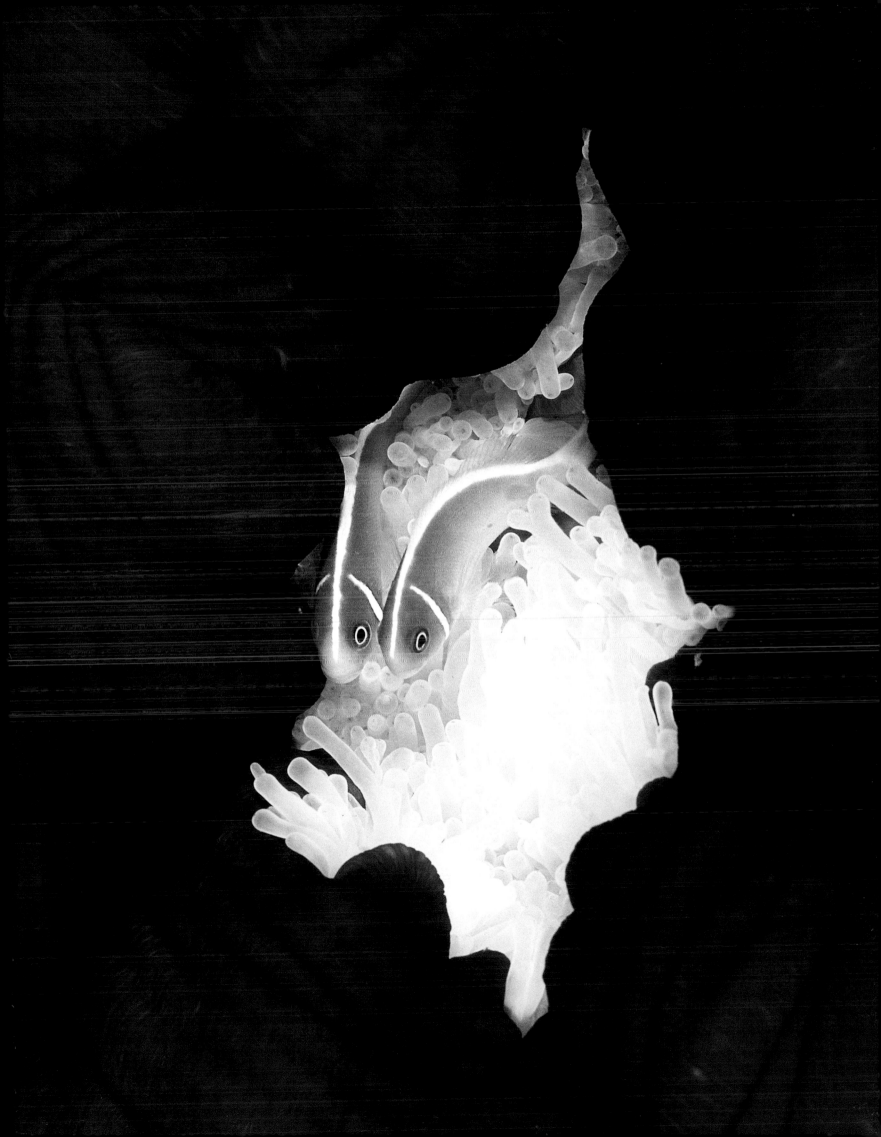

Clownfishes (also known as anemonefishes) are the classic example of symbiosis. They are immune to their host anemone's nematocysts – stinging cells that can paralyse other fish. This immunity is not hereditary, but acquired through what is known as acclimation behaviour. As soon as a young clownfish settles on an anemone, it starts rubbing itself against the anemone's tentacles. These are covered with a mucous coating, which contains a substance used to prevent the stimulation of a stinging reaction by the nematocysts, as the tentacles come into contact with one another. Gradually, the clownfish acquires a protective mucous coat and can move freely among the tentacles. As the fish comes into contact with the anemone, the nematocysts do not sting it, thinking that it is just another mucus-coated tentacle. In aquarium conditions, if a clownfish is separated from its host for too long, it loses its protective coat and when it is introduced back to the anemone it has to go through another acclimation period.

Divers often mistake the corallimorpharian *Amplexidiscus fenestrafer* for a sea anemone. Fish that decide to settle on it to spend the night are making a fatal mistake. As soon as the carnivorous corallimorpharian senses a meal, it uses its oral disk to envelop the fish. Once it has trapped its prey, it opens its mouth and swallows the fish, which is killed inside the coral polyp. Inexperienced aquarium owners who place this corallimorpharian together with fish in the same tank are likely to wake up one morning with fewer fish and a happy corallimorpharian.

In aquarium experiments, it has been observed that clownfishes sometimes also settle for the night on the corallimorpharian, as they would do on their host anemone, and are devoured. Is it safe to infer that this corallimorpharian mimics a host anemone in order to attract clownfish fry to settle and subsequently eat them? When its larval phase terminates, the clownfish settles on the sea floor and, within a day, acquires its juvenile colours. At this stage, it is imperative for the young clownfish to find a host anemone as soon as possible, to avoid being eaten. Some species locate their host by following the trail of chemicals released by the anemone. Others do not rely on chemical signals and seem to locate their host by chance or by sight. As a result, they might confuse a corallimorpharian with a host anemone, settle in and become prey. The hypothesis, however, has not been documented in natural conditions.

Left:
Periclimenes sp. on the sea star Culcita sp. There are more than 240 shrimp species, which are commensal on various hosts.

Right:
Corallimorpharian, Amplexidiscus fenestrafer (30cm).

Opposite: Divers become so fascinated while observing clownfish that they sometimes fail to notice the small spotted porcelain crab, Neopetrolisthes maculata (3cm), which may be found in the same anemone. The crabs, usually a male and a female, can move safely in and out of the anemone's mouth.

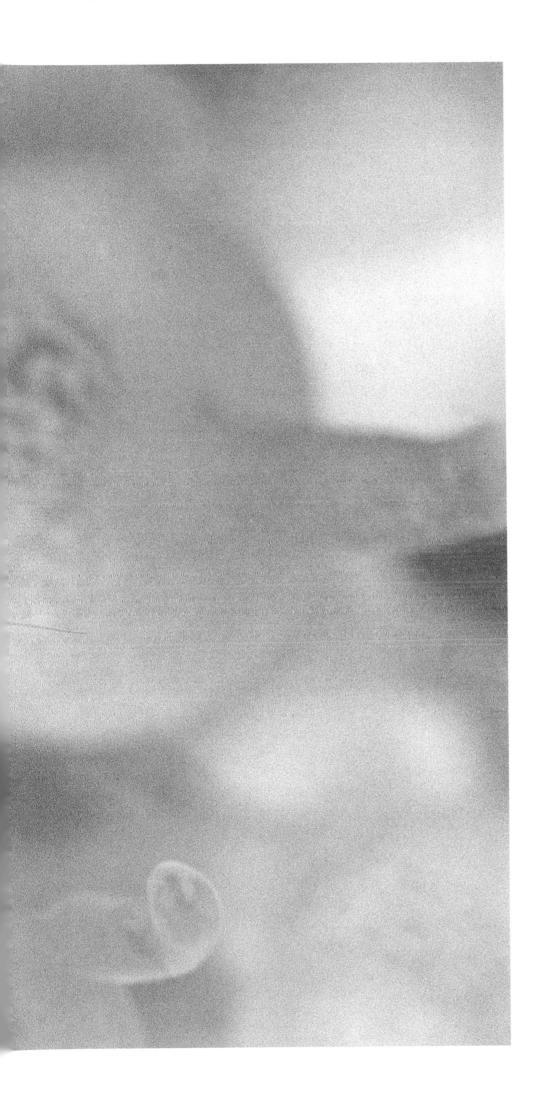

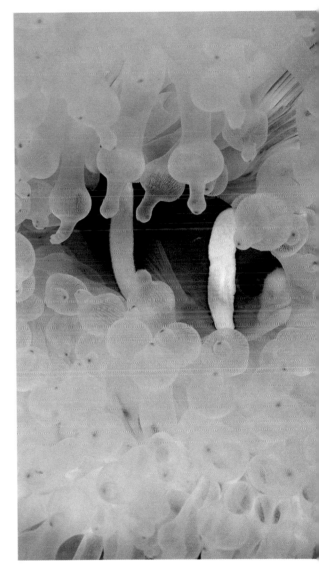

Above: Bleached sea anemone, Entacmaea quadricolor, with Clark's clownfish, Amphiprion clarkii (14cm).

Left: Bleached sea anemone, Entacmaea quadricolor, with commensal shrimp, Periclimenes holthuisi (2.5cm).

Overleaf: Bigfin reef squid at night, Sepioteuthis lessoniana (30cm). Squid swim much faster than cuttlefish due to their elongated and therefore streamlined bodies. Cuttlefish regulate their buoyancy with the cuttlebone, a lightweight, flat, calcareous shell located under the dorsal mantle tissue. In squid, the cuttlebone equivalent is the gladius, a gelatinous rod.

This page: Squat lobster, Galathea cf. spinosorostris (0.4cm).

Opposite: The tube guardian, Lissocarcinus laevis (1.5cm), lives in association with sea anemones and soft corals.

Reef-building (hermatypic) corals and sea anemones are an example of animal-plant symbiosis. Both contain single-celled microscopic algae, called zooxanthellae, in their tissues. Like all plants, zooxanthellae require sunlight for photosynthesis, whereby the algae uses solar energy, carbon dioxide, inorganic nutrients and water to produce carbon-enriched organic compounds. These compounds are used to feed the algae, but the majority leak to the coral or sea anemone, providing energy. In the case of hard corals, photosynthesis provides the majority of the polyp's nutritional requirements (see also Hermatypic Coral Nutrition in Notes & Abbreviations, p. 245). Therefore, those hard corals and anemones, containing zooxanthellae, need to be in clear, shallow water where there is ample sunlight. As depth increases, water filters out sunlight and, as a result, sea anemones are not encountered deeper than 50m.

Pollution, excessive warming of the water and increased ultraviolet radiation due to the depletion of the ozone layer cause stress to corals and anemones. In response the symbiotic animals expel the zooxanthellae from their tissues. The animal loses its colour, which is why this condition is called bleaching. This leads to starvation, since the presence of zooxanthellae is critical for the animal's nutrition. Depending on the species and stress level, the coral may withstand undernourishment for up to four weeks and will be able to recover if conditions improve. The tolerance of corals and anemones for temperature increases is limited to a couple of degrees Celsius above usual levels. The ideal temperature range for photosymbiotic hermatypic corals is 20-28/29°C. Reefs will not develop where winter temperatures drop below 18°C. For example, at 18°C a colony of *Pocillopora damicornis* dies in less than two weeks. If the temperature drops to 15°C, death occurs within a day.

The prolonged rise in temperatures due to the 1997-98 El Niño caused severe bleaching on many reefs around the world, from the Red Sea to the Great Barrier Reef in Australia. The most shocking example was the case of the Maldives, where more than 90% of all zooxanthellae dependents (sea anemones, corals and giant clams) suffered severe bleaching. In the Lembeh Strait I noticed no bleaching during my trip in 1997. When I arrived in December 1998 there were a few cases, but I had to look to find them. The bleached sea anemones in the pictures on the previous page is one example. By February, cold water upwellings brought by the strong currents dropped water temperature, creating the conditions necessary for recovery.

Coral reefs are affected by natural phenomena, such as hurricanes, and by human activity. Today, they are one of the world's most threatened habitats and nearly 60% are threatened by human activities such as: collection of corals and seashells for the tourist trade; pollution from sewage and fertilisers used in agriculture; pollution from oil; silting – as forests are cleared inland, rain washes the soil to the sea; destructive fishing methods (dynamite and cyanide fishing); overfishing; unregulated tourism – damage from anchors, trampling, litter; and global warming.

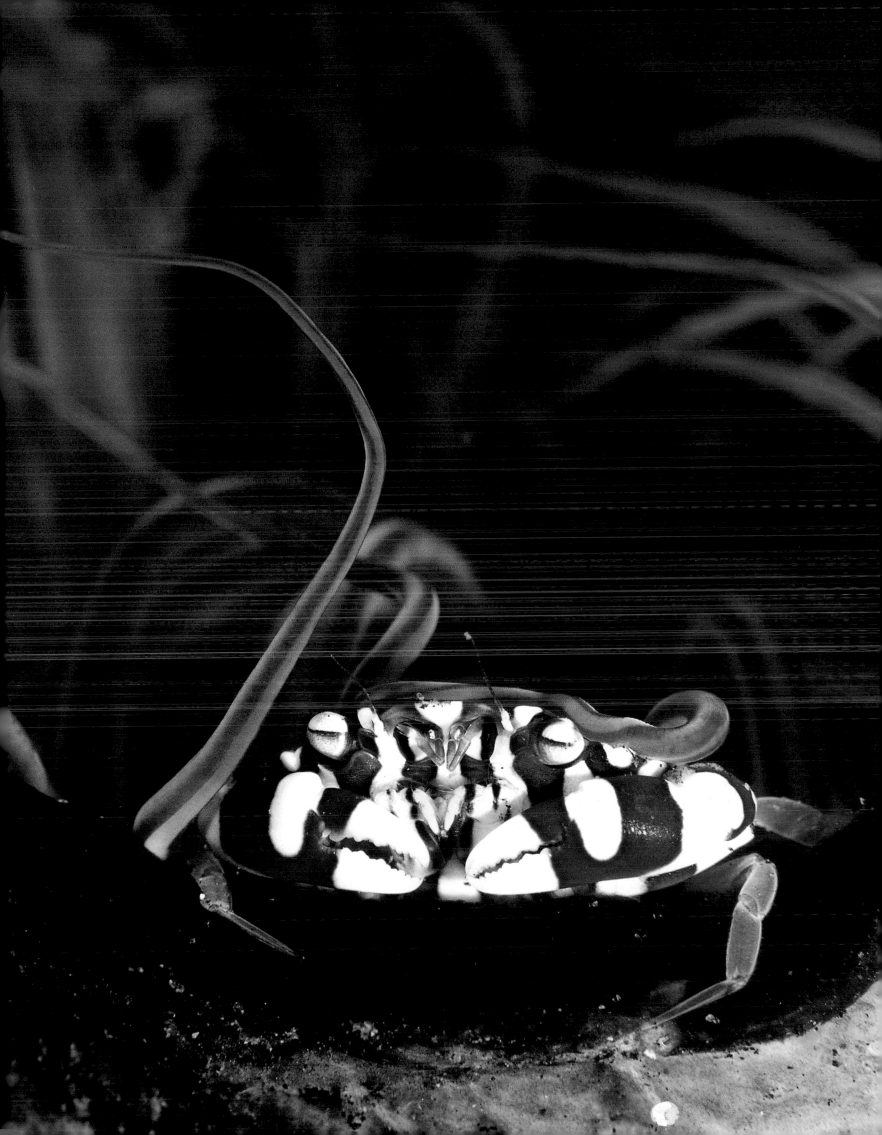

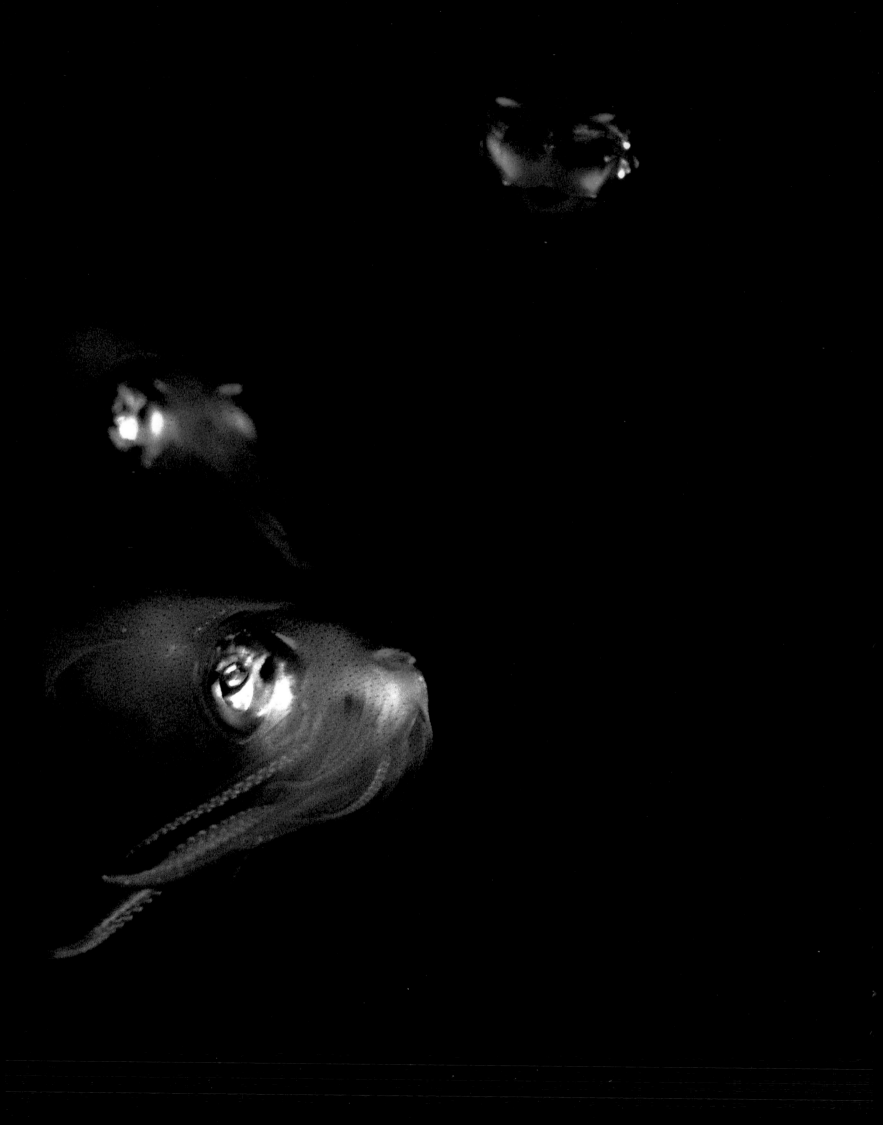

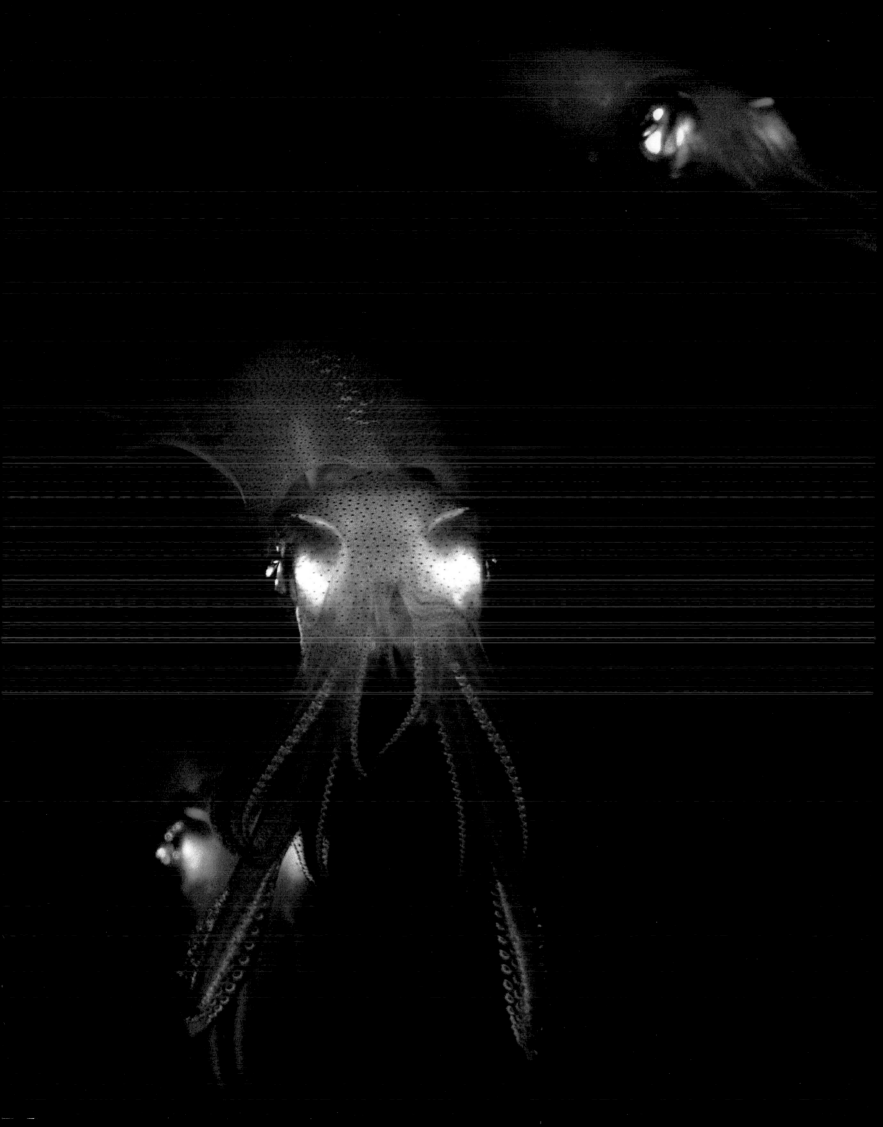

INNOVATIVE HOUSING CONCEPTS

Despite the vastness of the oceans, competition for housing is intense. Unfortunately for fish and divers, the geographical expansion of coral reefs – the architects of the sea – is generally restricted to the broad band that falls between the tropics of Cancer and Capricorn (23.5 degrees or 1410 nautical miles on either side of the Equator). However, thanks to warm ocean currents, there are isolated reefs outside this range – Bermuda (32.5° N), Lord Howe Island (31.5° S) and the islands outside Tokyo Bay (34° N). The main reason that coral reefs are limited to 600,000 square kilometres (about 0.2% of the world's ocean area) is that they require clear, warm, shallow water for photosynthesis and hence for nutrition and growth. Out of approximately 14,600 marine fishes, there are 7,000 species living in coral reefs. The diversity is astounding. Of course, there are quite a few species awaiting discovery. While I was at KBR, Takamasa 'Tono' Tonozuka, discovered a new wrasse species (*Labridae*), named *Cirrhilabrus tonozukai*. Tono discovered this species during a dive at *Nudi Falls*, depth 27m. Nus shrimp, a beautiful new species, was recently discovered by Nuswanto 'Nus' Lobbu.

Coral reefs are the largest living structures on earth. Reef-building corals settle in the shallows to have ample sunlight for photosynthesis. They then proceed to build the calcareous foundations of the coral reef metropolis. At the same time, numerous invertebrates and vertebrates move in, to claim a spot in the new city. This congregation in relatively small areas inevitably leads to housing shortages and some creatures are forced to find ingenious ways to house and protect themselves. Together with the reef metropolis, cities made out of human garbage appear here and there, a testimony to the fact that we still consider oceans an endless wastebasket. Today, chemical contamination and litter is widespread in the oceans, even at abyssal depths. Litter goes a bit further than your ordinary plastic bottle. Documentation exists of several nuclear warheads and nuclear reactors that have been lost at sea. Divers around the world come across litter on every single dive. Some of these items are slowly swallowed up by the reef and eventually contribute to its foundations, much like the shell of a dead clam. Others, such as empty cans, become artificial housing units. An empty can that is tossed overboard and lands on the sand becomes a valuable hideout for a freckled porcupinefish, *Diodon holocanthus*, which uses it much as it would use the central cavity of a barrel sponge. The can's lid makes a perfect roof cover for an octopus that has moved into a seashell (see photo 106 top). Needless to say, all these creatures, given the choice, would vote for clean and unpolluted seas. After all, would you choose to live in a city dump?

In the Lembeh Strait, *Hairball* is the dive site that has plenty of octopuses, some of which hide inside discarded tin cans. During a dive at *Hairball*, I decided to check the various cans for octopuses. I was surprised when I found a painted frogfish, *Antennarius pictus*, in one of them (see photos p. 106-107). The can had two holes: one on the top and one on its side. What a perfect spot for this small frogfish (about 8cm) to ambush its prey. Although frogfishes are known to maintain the same position, this one displayed great mobility. Initially, its head protruded from the top hole. I saw it use its lure to catch a small fish in a split-second move that was impossible to photograph. Moments later, it ate another fish. Given this success, I didn't expect the frogfish to abandon its prime fishing location. Nonetheless, it moved to the hole on the side, settled down again and started using its lure. A passing shrimp disappeared. The frogfish kept fishing into the night.

This page: Sharpsnout snake eel, Apterichthus klazingai (40cm). This is a very secretive species that spends most of its time buried in the sand. Unlike the ribbon eel (Muraenidae), snake eels (Ophichthidae) do not build a burrow. Instead, they use the rigid tip of their tail to slide tail first under the sand or mud.

Opposite: A freckled porcupine fish, Diodon holocanthus (29cm) hides inside an empty can as it would do with a barrel sponge.

This page top: Veined or margined octopus, Octopus marginatus (30cm). Its improvised home consists of a sea shell with the lid of a tin can for a roof.

This page bottom & opposite: Painted frogfish, Antennarius pictus (10cm), using a tin can as an ambush site. A portrait of this frogfish can also be seen on page 30.

A tennis shoe seems like a good anemone substitute for the clownfish, *Amphiprion polymnus*, opposite to spend the night. Here is the story. I had noticed the tennis shoe during the day while observing an overcrowded sea anemone, *Stichodactyla haddoni*. During the night dive, as I was casually checking the anemone, I noticed this saddleback anemonefish resting on the tennis shoe rather than on its host. I was perplexed by this behaviour and checked the KBR library. Clownfishes live in matriarchal societies that observe a strict social hierarchy. The largest fish is the dominant female and the next largest is her mate. The adult pair lives in harmony. However, the male must maintain its privileged position in order to pass its genes on to the next generation. Therefore, it is aggressive towards any challengers, particularly its aspiring successor, the next largest male. As we move down the social ladder, each individual strives to maintain and possibly increase its social status. However, once a newcomer appears, individuals forget their personal differences and unite in their efforts to expel the intruder. The latter must fight vigorously to become accepted, otherwise he must find another anemone before he falls victim to a predator. This tennis-shoe squatter was probably not an unwelcome intruder, since he kept returning to his host during the day (clownfish numbers on the particular anemone remained unchanged). In this case, the clownfish had probably drifted with the current at night and settled on the nearby tennis shoe. Waking up in a different bed in the morning must have been a surprise!

Many reef animals need to construct a burrow in order to survive. In fact, there are some serious architects in the underwater world. Snapping shrimps, *Alpheidae*, are renowned for constructing and maintaining goby burrows. The goby positions itself at the entrance to the burrow while the shrimp brings out sand and rubble much like a caterpillar tractor. The shrimp empties its load outside the construction site, shifts into reverse gear and retreats inside the burrow, tail first. It has poor vision and its safety depends on the goby that is on the lookout for predators. Therefore, when venturing outside the burrow, the shrimp maintains physical contact with its guardian angel at all times, using its long antennae. When the goby senses danger, it alerts the shrimp with a rapid fluttering of its tail. If the photographer persists, the goby moves backward to the entrance of the burrow. At this stage, you need to step back to make the goby feel safe, otherwise it will spin around and disappear head first into the burrow. As the goby darts inside, the walls partly collapse. It will take some time for the goby to feel safe enough to re-emerge. The snapping shrimp will then start its endless task of maintaining the burrow's structure all over again. Wouldn't you like to have someone clean up your mess again and again without complaining?

The ribbon eel, *Rhinomuraena quaesita*, is a master builder. It builds its burrow in the sand, mud or coral rubble. This moray species is diurnal and prefers to hunt from the safety of its burrow, feeding on small fishes. Despite the fact that mature females may reach 130cm in length, you are likely to see only the head and a portion of the body protruding from the hole. Skittish by nature, the ribbon eel retracts inside its burrow at the slightest sign of danger. As it moves up and down inside its lair, one would expect its scaleless body, characteristic of all moray eels, to be full of cuts and abrasions from the rough surfaces of the burrow walls. However, the eel's skin remains unaffected, thanks to the mucus produced by cells located on the skin of its belly. This mucus works much like the plaster used in home construction. It bonds the various particles together, resulting in smooth, tube-like burrow walls. The benefit is twofold: protection for the eel's scaleless skin and a solidly constructed burrow. I imagine that an empty ribbon eel burrow would immediately fall into the reef's prime real-estate category. Unfortunately, this popular aquarium species is often collected using cyanide.

This page: Snapping shrimp, Alpheus bellulus (4cm). The common name is derived from the snapping sound these shrimps can make with their larger pincer, called major chela.

Saddleback anemonefish, Amphiprion polymnus (12cm), using a tennis shoe as an anemone substitute.

This page: Pelagic swimming crab, Portunus pelagicus (20cm), and Savigny's sea urchin, Diadema savignyi.
Opposite: A mooring line provides a perfect ambush site for this frogfish, Antennarius sp.

In contrast to the ribbon eel, other species of the moray eel family do not construct a burrow. Instead, they set up their house inside a reef crevice, which they leave at night or during the day, depending on whether they are nocturnal or diurnal, to forage for food. The moray eel is a formidable predator. With its keen sense of smell, it can locate even those animals that seek shelter inside deep reef fissures. Its serpentine and muscular body enables it to squeeze into the crack and capture its prey. As a moray eel moves over the reef inspecting the various holes for little crustaceans or a delicious octopus, its skin is exposed to very rough treatment. To prevent abrasions, the skin is about five times thicker than that of scaled fish. Mucus glands in the epidermis exude copious amounts of slime to protect the body from parasites. Cleaner shrimps favour morays, not only for their parasites, but also because their nutrient-rich mucus is a real treat.

Like all creatures, moray eels need to breathe to survive. To do so, they must keep their mouth open to enable the muscles in the gill cavity to pump fresh water over the gills. This exposes their formidable teeth and makes them look ferocious and menacing, despite the fact that they are actually rather shy by nature. Of course, like all animals, including humans, morays will defend themselves if threatened or provoked. I must admit that I feel very little sympathy for any spear fisherman who is bitten while trying to kill a moray.

The mutilated swimming crab hiding under debris on page 115 (middle) has lost four limbs, both chelipeds and two left legs. It has had a fierce encounter with a predator and managed to escape by self-amputation! There is a special breakage point at the base of every leg that connects the limb to the main body. The crab used muscular action to separate the leg, while a diaphragm sealed the wound to prevent blood loss. Crabs are able to regenerate the amputated limbs and move on with their life. This crab faces two challenges: it must escape predation, despite being a cripple, and it must feed without claws. Its future seems rather precarious. Notice the moray protruding from the debris. It was not difficult for the eel, with its keen sense of smell, to detect the injured crab. But is it too big a prey for the tiny moray? Self-amputation is a last resort escape option for many crustaceans.

The octopus, an intelligent and resourceful animal, never ceases to amaze me. I was very surprised when, during a night dive, I found a veined octopus, *Octopus marginatus*, using a seashell for cover (see photo p. 117). Octopuses prey on snails by drilling holes into the shell and then injecting their saliva so as to weaken the muscle, separate it from the shell and consume the mollusc. However, since the shell was intact, it was probably already empty when the octopus found it. I sat there observing the great dexterity with which the octopus was opening and closing the shell. Despite being bigger than the shell, it had no problem squeezing inside its improvised home.

The veined octopus is a common sight, but this unusual behaviour made it a special photo opportunity. I decided to stay and observe it. However, the octopus was also checking me out and, after a while, decided it was best to move away to a safer distance. It opened the shell, placed its feet outside and started walking on the sand while carrying its improvised home along with it! Unfortunately, as soon as I got close enough to compose a picture, the octopus went back inside the shell. A photographer must always move away immediately if he sees that his presence is causing an animal stress. This will, hopefully, make the subject feel less threatened and allow it to continue its routine, perhaps even giving the photographer a second chance. I moved away and waited for five minutes. I then tried to move closer, as quietly as possible, but the octopus took the shell and moved away again. It was clear that I had somehow upset it and that it was not comfortable in my presence.

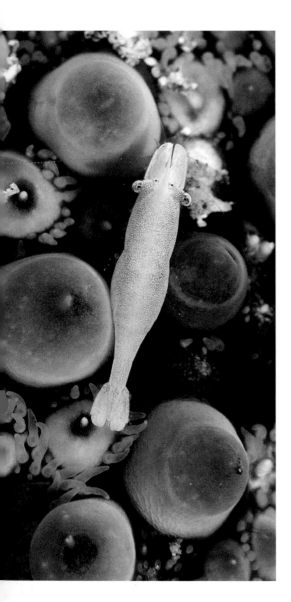

This starfish shrimp, Periclimenes soror (1.3cm), is commensal on several sea star species such as Acanthaster, Culcita, Choriaster and Linckia. Its colour varies from tan to purple, matching the colour of its host.

This page: White-eyed moray, Siderea thyrsoidea (66cm), and sea star, Linckia laevigata (40cm).

Page 114: Imperial shrimp, Periclimenes imperator (2cm), on sea cucumber

Page 115 top: Snowflake moray, Echidna nebulosa (70cm), hiding among the arms of a sea star, Choriaster granulatus (30cm).

Page 115 middle: Mutilated swimming crab and tiny moray eel.

Page 115 bottom: Unidentified moray eel.

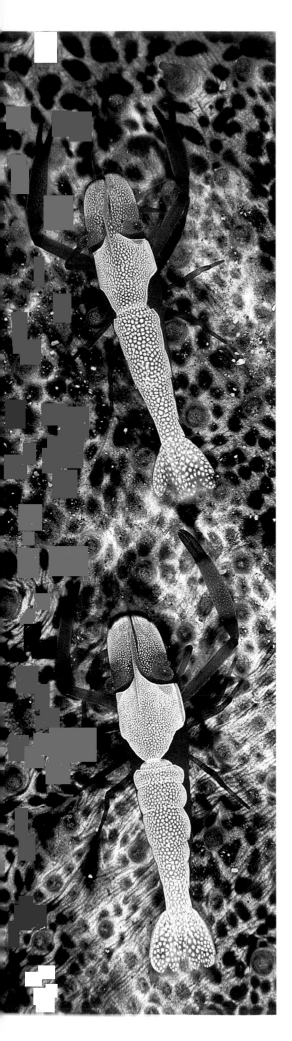

Of course, the shell is not a typical octopus home. Usually, an octopus finds a suitable crevice among the rocks, moves in and then gathers various pebbles around the entrance. After a while, its lair can be easily identified by the crustacean debris that is scattered nearby. It generally spends its day inside its den and comes out at night to hunt. Once the octopus senses danger, it will retract inside its hole, dragging a few small stones with the suction cups on its feet, thus closing the entrance to the den. Luring an octopus from the safety of its lair is not easy, even if you place food right outside. As it is inquisitive by nature, the octopus will want to examine the food and you will notice it getting agitated. However, it seems to be aware that 'curiosity kills the cat'. Instead of abandoning its den at the first sight of food, it will cautiously extend one of its arms, feel the food with its sensitive suckers and, if it is to its liking, bring it inside the den for consumption.

In the Greek islands, fishermen have found various ways to lure and catch the *Octopus vulgaris* during the day, to satisfy the insatiable appetite of residents and tourists alike for grilled octopus and ouzo (see photo p. 122). A common technique is based on the belief that the octopus is attracted to the colour white. The fisherman slowly drags along the bottom of the sea a small piece of white cloth, to lure the octopus out of its den. As soon as he feels resistance, he pulls the fishing line, hoping to catch the octopus with the big hook that lies between the folds of the white cloth. He then has to pull very fast, before the octopus can find a steady hold among the rocks with its suction cups. However, the octopus can and frequently does outsmart the fisherman. As it is being pulled to the surface, it finds the time to use its strong legs to free itself from the hook. It is actually quite a funny scene to watch. The fisherman swears and curses at the sight of the escaping octopus and, when his blood pressure returns to normal, asks forgiveness from the Virgin Mary. He then starts rowing again and the process repeats itself until an octopus is caught.

While in Indonesia, I frequently observed a subsistence fisherman fishing for octopus in the shallows during the daytime. One day he displayed with pride a big *Octopus cyanea*.

'What technique do you use to catch the octopus?' I asked in flawless Indonesian, translated by Nuswanto. 'I drag this piece of cloth on the sea floor...' etc. 'But why do you use a brown cloth? The fishermen in my country use a white cloth.' 'That is wrong,' he replied. 'The octopus is attracted to the colour brown because it thinks it is a conspecific and comes out to mate.'

That's an interesting theory. So where does the truth lie, white or brown? Is the octopus attracted to the colour or is the dangling in itself enough to attract its curiosity, irrespective of colour? Probably the latter, since the structure of their eyes suggests that most cephalopods are colour-blind. So much for the prized secrets of Greek and Indonesian fishermen!

Another fishing technique capitalises on the octopus's housing preferences. Containers of all shapes and sizes end up daily in the oceans. If you were an octopus, would you prefer to squeeze yourself into the tight quarters of a rock crevice or the spacious accommodation of a tin can? Would you go for the apartment or the villa? The octopus definitely opts for the villa and is known to occupy various discarded containers. I have seen fishermen attach a series of plastic containers to a line and sink them to the sea floor. When retrieved after a couple of days, most containers had an octopus inside. As a rule of thumb while diving, always check any containers for octopuses.

The octopus must face many predators, such as seals, sharks, groupers, moray eels and, of course, humans. The Japanese prefer it raw whereas Greeks pound the octopus exactly 40 times – a fisherman's magic number – to tenderise the flesh and then boil it.

This page: Broadclub cuttlefish, Sepia latimanus (50cm).

Opposite: Veined or margined octopus, Octopus marginatus, (30cm) using a seashell for shelter.

Page 118 top: Eye detail of a broadclub cuttlefish, Sepia latimanus (50cm).

Page 118 middle: Eye detail of a bigfin reef squid, Sepioteuthis lessoniana (30cm).

Page 118 bottom: Eye detail of an Octopus cyanea (40cm)

Page 119: Bobtail squid, Eupyrmna morsei (8cm). This diminutive cephalopod is a nocturnal species. It buries itself under the rubble during the day, using its two tentacles to toss various particles over its body. The particles stay in place thanks to a mucous coating produced by a special gland in the epidermis. The bobtail squid emerges at night to feed on small crustacea. Note the biologically generated light – bioluminescence – which is produced in special light organs called photophores. These organs have an uneven distribution on the animal's body. There are usually more photophores on the underside than on the back. In cephalopods, light organs are common under the eye and there are more on the ventral than on the dorsal side of the mantle. Bioluminescence is a widespread phenomenon among marine organisms, cephalopods, crustaceans and fishes. It is used for ventral counter-illumination and signalling.

Alternatively, they let it dry in the sun, a common sight in the Greek islands, and then prepare it on the grill. In their short lifespan – about two years for most species – octopuses and other cephalopods have to use deception to avoid being eaten. The key to survival is to become invisible by changing their colour to blend with the environment. If this technique – known as crypsis – fails, then the cephalopod must resort to secondary defence. If it senses danger, a squid may disappear by swimming fast and an octopus can retreat inside the smallest crack, provided it matches the size of its beak. If the beak can go through then so will the rest of the animal! Alternatively, the cephalopod may use colour change to threaten, startle, confuse or frighten the predator (deimatic behaviour). If this fails, it will attempt an unpredictable and erratic escape (protean behaviour). In this case, squirting ink works either as a decoy that distracts the predator's attention or as a smokescreen that obscures his vision, creating a window of opportunity for the cephalopod to escape. The animal uses its funnel, also called a siphon, to expel water forcibly, generating jet propulsion. Steering is achieved by repositioning the muscular siphon in the right direction. The ink is produced by a gland inside the mantle that surrounds the internal organs and expelled through the siphon, situated on the edge of the ventral mantle. In general, cephalopods have a large well-developed brain, acute eyesight and quick movements. As a result, they can assess a predator's intentions ahead of time and have several defence options available.

How do cephalopods change their skin pigmentation for deimatic display or in order to match their surroundings? The secret lies in millions of chromatophore cells located under the cephalopod's skin. Think of them as a five-colour (yellow, orange, red, brown and black) inkjet printer. When the surrounding muscles receive the order 'print' from the highly evolved nervous system, they squeeze the chromatophore cells, which expand, thus producing colour. Otherwise, the muscles are relaxed and the cephalopod has a pale colour. In general, a cephalopod can change skin colour and texture faster than any animal on land. Its skin is normally smooth. Muscles in the dermis can instantly give it a highly papillated texture (see photo p. 120). As a result, a cephalopod can change colour, texture and shape and use the resulting body patterns for crypsis or communication. Octopuses use cryptic colouration to merge their outline with the colour of their surroundings and cryptic behaviour to mimic plants or animals and deceive their predators. Unlike cuttlefishes, which use colour change to communicate during courtship, octopuses have poor intraspecific signalling. If you are lucky enough to spot an octopus during the daytime, follow it from a distance and you will be mesmerised by its graceful movements and body patterns.

How intelligent is an octopus? Octopuses have a large brain, an extensive nervous system and the ability to learn by observation. They are sensitive and emotional. Some studies consider them as intelligent as a cat. It is worth mentioning an experiment conducted at the Monterey Bay Aquarium to test octopus memory and learning ability. Researchers placed two octopus tanks side by side. Into one tank they introduced two square metal plates, one black and one white. When an octopus touched the white plate it received an electric shock; when it touched the black, it received food. It took several trials before the octopuses learned to touch only the black plate. Then, the researchers replaced the octopuses with those that had been in the adjacent tank. These animals, having observed the tests with their keen eyesight, knew immediately that they had to touch the black plate to obtain food. They never made the mistake of touching the white plate. Experiments have proved that octopuses learn faster by example and observation, i.e. by watching other octopuses perform a task, than through human training.

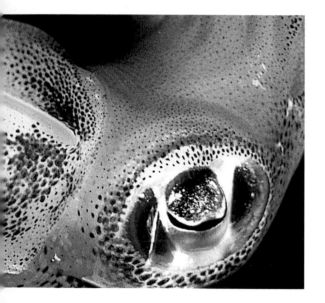

This page: Octopus cyanea (40cm). Notice the spiky texture of the skin.
Opposite: Broadclub cuttlefish, Sepia latimanus (50cm).

Divers come to the Lembeh Strait to see two recently discovered and undescribed octopus species, the wonderpus and the mimic octopus. Our dive guide told us that he had located a wonderpus burrow at *Aer Parang* and that it was guaranteed that we would see the elusive creature emerge at exactly 5 p.m. I thought he was pulling our leg, but everybody else was so excited at the prospect of seeing the wonderpus that I was forced to perform the ultimate sacrifice: skip a night dive in favour of a dusk dive. We all knelt in a semi-circle on the sandy bottom and waited. At exactly 5p.m., nothing happened and I wished I had my slate with me so that I could write, 'I told you so!' However, five minutes later, a fabulous creature emerged from its burrow. I was mesmerised. After a few flashes the animal made a deimatic display by flaring its arms to increase its volume (see photo p. 125). I took a few shots and then stepped back, complying with the dive guide's instructions. Seeing that its deimatic display bore fruit, the wonderpus continued its hunting rounds for crustaceans.

The five o' clock 'trick' worked again on subsequent days, because the wonderpus needs to come out at dusk to feed. After a while, once the crustacean stocks of the immediate area were depleted, it relocated its burrow to a new, untamed territory. Although this undescribed octopus resembles the famous mimic octopus, it is most probably a different species.

The Lembeh Strait acquired its reputation from a number of unusual animals but its fame skyrocketed following the discovery of the pygmy seahorse and, lately, of the mimic octopus. Film crews rushed to the Strait to film the various mimic octopus impersonations. I was able to photograph the elusive octopus in the course of a drift dive from *Aw Shucks* towards *Hairball*. Needless to say, I was devastated when a major international courier company damaged all my mimic octopus images, along with 1,358 slides. Although these were crucial photographs, I still had over 25,000 slides to choose for the book. As the book was ready to go to press and, having spent over a year stuck in my office, I decided to take a much-needed break. I made a trip to Bali and dove in Secret Bay, a muck dive site similar to *Hairball* or *Aer Parang* in the Lembeh Strait. During one dive, Akira Ogawa found a mimic octopus and I was able to take some unique behavioural pictures.

'Stop the presses! Stop the presses!' I shouted to the book's designer over the phone. She tried to reason with the lunatic on the other end, but in vein. I wanted to include these mimic octopus pictures in here in order to give a more complete picture to the diver that plans to visit the Lembeh Strait. After all, this octopus species is a star attraction of the Strait. Here is the account of my mimic octopus experience.

The octopus had two burrows in close proximity. The burrows are not interconnected but they provide alternative hideouts when the animal is outside its burrow and needs to disappear quickly because of a predator. It was apparent that, when the octopus was out hunting, it remained in the immediate vicinity of the two alternative burrows. Only after having finished checking the surrounding area did it move further away. The burrow was obviously the point of reference at all times. Akira Ogawa noticed the octopus as it protruded from its burrow (see photo p. 127). We knelt on the sand and waited patiently. I was observing the octopus from quite some distance. I was afraid to move closer to take a picture, because I was certain that such a bold move would scare off the octopus making it disappear. My reservations were based on numerous encounters with the *Octopus vulgaris* in the Mediterranean. However, Akira insisted that it was safe for me to move in for a shot. I approached the octopus with extreme caution and took a portrait shot. How surprising! The octopus seemed to be completely oblivious to my presence. It did not give the slightest sign of wanting to retreat inside its burrow. As a rule, the *Octopus vulgaris* usually retreats immediately, to

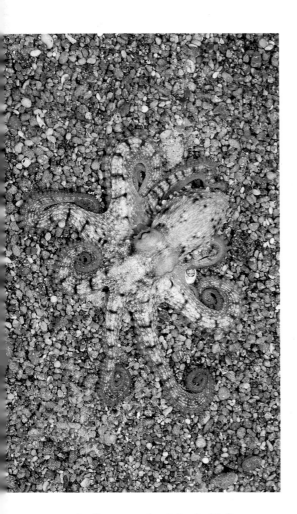

An Octopus vulgaris in the Mediterranean demonstrates its ability to blend perfectly with the background.

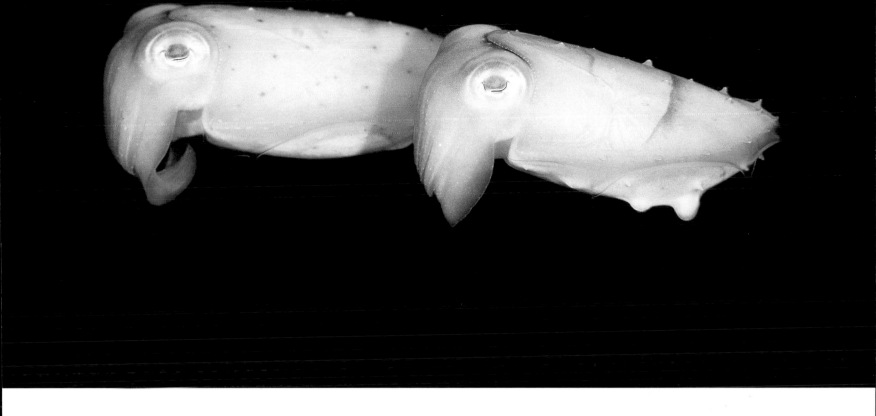

Top: *Juvenile broadclub cuttlefish, Sepia latimanus (50cm). The adult is pictured on pages 49, 116 and 121. In contrast to the octopus (Gr: eight legs), cuttlefish and squid are decapods - that is, they have ten arms.*

Bottom; *Flamboyant cuttlefish, Metasepia pfefferi (12cm).*

be on the safe side. Yet the mimic was not at all preturbed and I was able to secure a few more shots before slowly distancing myself. Eventually, the octopus emerged from its lair and began its hunting rounds. Once more, I was surprised by the fact that we - three divers - were swimming right above the octopus and it simply did not care. Even when I approached to photograph it, there was no change whatsoever in its course. How strange! In general, the octopus is a very intelligent animal, with keen eyesight, and it can easily spot a diminutive shrimp, let alone an approaching diver weighing 100 kilos. In fact, the wonderpus on the opposite page immediately flared its arms as I approached to take a photograph. So what about the mimic? Why was it so unafraid of an approaching potential predator? One can make several assumptions. It might be poisonous and therefore unafraid. Or maybe because I was overcautious in my approach, I did not stress this particular individual at all and it was comfortable in my presence. Whatever the reason, the animal was not stressed at all and I had the pleasure to observe its hunting technique repeatedly.

The octopus was moving on the sandy bottom, legs outstretched, feeling every minuscule hole. Numerous tiny shrimps and crabs - some barely visible - were fleeing from its path. Pure terror! Nowhere to hide! At the time, I compared it to a war scene, with a tank advancing into a city and powerless civilians running for their lives. I was expecting the mimic to jet forward and form a fishing net with its legs to capture the fleeing animals. In retrospect, the mimic has a much better chance of capturing its prey when ambushed inside a burrow rather than while running around in the open with several escape options available. Indeed, most predators will not waste energy to pursue their prey when their presence has been detected and the odds are against them. The octopus kept using its sensitive legs to probe the substrate for food. Suddenly, it formed a net with its legs (much like the wonderpus on page 53) and moments later it rushed back to its den. Once again it stayed with half its body protruding from the hole but, this time, the muscle tension of its legs revealed that it was trying to consume some sort of prey. Was it a crab? A shrimp perhaps? A mollusc? We did not have to wait long to find out. The octopus used its siphon to discard the shells of a small bivalve, ate the animal and resumed its hunting rounds. This time it approached a log buried under the sand. I noticed that there were two holes on either side of the log, probably entry and exit points to a burrow. The octopus had obviously made a similar assessment. With swift movements, it went over the log while simultaneously extending its legs inside both openings. The octopus knew that it had to block all escape routes to get its next meal. Suddenly, a big swimming crab jumped out brandishing its claws. It used its paddles (modified fifth, or last, pair of legs) to swim away. At the same time, the octopus having been pinched by the startled crab changed its colour to dark brown and flared its legs (see photos p. 128-129). The octopus took on its pale colour and resumed its search for food. Back to the burrow with a new bivalve. This time, however, things got complicated. As soon as the octopus discarded the two shells, a fire worm emerged from an adjacent tiny burrow. It moved right up to the octopus and ventured under its legs to steal its food! The mimic changed colour, but the fire worm was not intimidated. It kept probing under the octopus' legs for food. The latter seemed totally powerless to deal with the situation. It used two legs to try to push the fire worm away but the worm persisted (see photos p. 130-131). Did it manage to steal a morsel before the octopus consumed the mollusc? The fire worm decided to go and check the discarded shells for leftovers and then disappeared inside its burrow.

The mimic octopus left and returned with its third bivalve. Once again, the moment it managed to separate the two shells, the fire worm emerged from its burrow and the story repeated itself. Only this time, the fire worm was even bolder, and after challenging the octopus for a share in its meal, it remained in the vicinity. The agitated

Opposite: Wonderpus, Octopus sp. (25cm), making a deimatic display by flaring its legs to increase its volume. After making its rounds, it disappeared inside its burrow - a beak-sized hole in the sand. Theoretically, an octopus could easily enter through your nostril. A great idea for a science-fiction movie (rights available).

This page: Octopus cyanea (40cm). Many octopuses and other cephalopods are able to change colour as a form of self-defence. This behaviour is described as deimatic. According to R.T. Hanlon and J.B. Messenger, 'Deimatic displays [in cephalopods] are characterised by the sudden appearance of bold light/dark chromatic components, usually with spreading of arms, web or fins to create the illusion of largeness.' In octopuses, this display is complemented by the forcible blowing of water, using the siphon, at the approaching predator. Notice the two dark eye rings that characterise deimatic display.

Opposite: A mimic octopus impersonating a mantis shrimp or simply sitting at the entrance of its burrow and observing the surroundings before starting its hunting rounds?

This page: Sea grasses have roots and flowers, which are pollinated underwater. Much like sponges, sea grass meadows are often overlooked by divers finning to get to the colourful corals as fast as possible. Yet, like mangroves, sea grass fields form important nursery grounds for many juvenile fishes seeking shelter. They offer crucial protection from predators until the juveniles become of age and capable to face the challenges of the open ocean. This juvenile batfish, Platax teira (60cm), was photographed hiding among sea grasses growing at less than two metres of water. Sea grasses prefer the shallows where they can take advantage of the ample sunlight for photosythesis.

octopus kept monitoring the movements of the fire worm. Given the presence of the intruder, the mimic showed signs of hesitation about whether to stay and guard its burrow or leave to fetch another meal. Hunger prevailed and the octopus moved away while keeping a worried eye on the developments back home. It stopped on a nearby boulder to have a last look and make sure that everything was in order before moving away to hunt. The fire worm seized the opportunity to venture inside the octopus' burrow and inspect it. Even from a distance, the octopus spotted the fire worm immediately - proof of its excellent eyesight. It looked furious and rushed back to the burrow. As it approached, the fire worm was leaving and so there was no opportunity to see how it would deal with the situation if the worm had decided to stay inside. The fire worm returned to its own hole. A nerve-racking cat-and-mouse situation had developed. The mimic octopus sat at the entrance of its burrow and seemed unwilling to move given the presence of the fire worm. We decided to leave. After all we had been observing the octopus for over two hours (the depth was only four metres) and I had taken more shots that I ever expected. In the next couple of days, despite my spending several hours waiting by its burrow, the mimic octopus did not emerge. Either it had had enough to eat or it relocated to a new untamed territory to avoid being pestered by the audacious fire worm.

The mimic octopus derives its common name from accounts that it is able to mimic, among others, a feather star, a flounder (see photo p. 133), a sea snake, a cuttlefish and a stingray (see photo p. 132). It could be that this intelligent animal uses its keen eyesight and its ability to learn by observation and memory to mimic the shape and colour of other species. However, to date, there is no conclusive evidence to substantiate the mimicry abilities of this undescribed octopus species.

According to T.M. Gosliner & D.W. Behrens, 'Mimicry in the terrestrial environment… is well documented…. However, there are few documented cases of mimicry in the marine environment, with even less experimental evidence to support anecdotal accounts of its existence…. It should be emphasised that mimicry in…most marine invertebrates…is poorly known and is only now in the descriptive phase. As a result the study of mimicry in these organisms suffers from the lack of experimental rigor that characterises the study of terrestrial organisms.'

Certainly, a study that documents the mimicry attributed to the mimic octopus will be a major scientific breakthrough. However, it is highly unlikely that scientists will be able to analyse the aspects of this complex behaviour in the near future. In the meantime, while they struggle in laboratories, if you happen to be in the Lembeh Strait, just let your imagination go wild!

Unfortunately, with all the commotion about the mimic octopus, there is a rising demand for the aquarium market. Cyanide is the only way to get the octopus out of its burrow. Once captured, the mimic octopus will not survive long in the hands of its proud owner. I am told that before dying the octopus releases the absorbed cyanide through its skin and, as a result, the aquarium enthusiast ends up with a lot of dead fish. Even if one manages to acquire a mimic octopus that was captured without cyanide, the animal would die of starvation since, according to experts, it is impossible to feed such an animal in the confined quarters of an aquarium.

Tales about the impersonations of the mimic octopus have reached legendary proportions, comparable to seafarers' tales about giant squid engulfing whole ships. Do not be disappointed if you do not see this elusive creature. There are so many things to enjoy in the Lembeh Strait or any other dive destination. However, if the octopus does show up, relax and savour the experience like you would enjoy watching any other magnificent marine creature. Well… there is of course the added pleasure of telling other divers over a beer and watching them go green. And I thought that only octopuses changed colours…

The mimic octopus hunting. Notice how it uses its legs to block all possible escape routes of its prey.

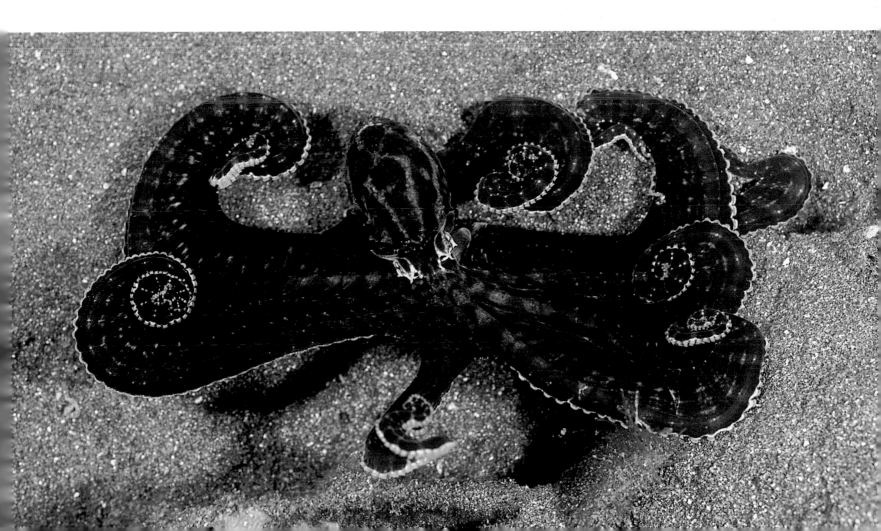

Throughout the fascinating sequence of events described in the main body of the text, it was apparent that the fire worm was in total control of the situation and that the mimic octopus was unable to drive away the intruder. There is speculation that the mimic octopus might be poisonous. Yet, if it is so, in this instance it was unable to use its poison against the intruder even while they were in close contact. Or perhaps it is not poisonous after all. At the same time, the octopus seemed unaffected by the fire worm's needle-like bristles - called setae - that can inflict a painful sting on humans.

In the Mediterranean, it is easy to locate an Octopus vulgaris from the leftovers around its den (crab carcasses, shells, etc). The octopus is often seen sitting at the entrance of its burrow, holding shells and pebbles with the suction cups on its legs. In contrast, the mimic octopus made an effort to distance the incriminating evidence - the shells - from the crime scene and thus avoid betraying the location of its burrow. After splitting a bivalve's shells, it used its siphon to jet them away and then it extended one leg to distance them even further. Still, at the end of our dive, there were three pairs of bivalve shells in the vicinity of the burrow. But, when I checked the burrow the next day, the shells had disappeared. Is it safe to infer that the mimic octopus had moved them further away to avoid attracting attention to the burrow's entrance? Possibly. If so, this action is definitely indicative of its intelligence.

A mimic octopus impersonating a stingray and a flounder? Apparently the mimic octopus will impersonate another animal - aggressive mimicry - in order to confuse a potential predator. However, there was definitely no sign whatsoever of a predator in the vicinity when the octopus assumed these shapes. There were three of us, of course, i.e. three big fish, but as I mention in the main text, we had not stressed the animal at all and this was demonstrated by the fact that it carried out three hunting expeditions in our presence. Had we been perceived as a threat, it would have disappeared in its burrow rather than repeatedly exposing itself in the open. So why did the mimic octopus assume the shape of a stingray? Maybe because it was simply using its legs to create a fishing net to capture its prey.

What about the flounder trick? Octopuses use jet propulsion to move. The particular octopus I was observing used jet propulsion to return quickly to its burrow whenever it had captured its prey. When hunting, the mimic octopus moves slowly, inspecting the sand inch by inch. However, once it has captured its meal, there is no need to risk staying out in the open. Jet propulsion is the fastest way to get it back to the safety of its burrow. Given its flexible body, the legs trail behind the head, giving a streamlined shape to the animal. This is a common form of locomotion among all octopuses. Some may view it as a flounder impersonation. But, when you are out hunting, you do not want to look like an animal that hunts in a similar way or has common predators. I see it as a form of locomotion. After all, let me stress that other than naturalist observations, such as mine, there is not a single published scientific paper on the behaviour of the mimic octopus.

REEF SEX

Octopuses mate by the male passing small thread-like packets of sperm called spermatophores to the female. The male's third right arm, the hectocotylus, is specially modified with a small spoon-like tip, called a ligula, and a gutter-like groove along the trailing edge. When mating, males send an arm into the gill cavity of the female and insert the tip into one of her two oviducts. They then use their penis to place a spermatophore into the groove at the base of their special arm. The spermatophore is shunted along this groove to the arm tip and into the female's oviduct. There, it turns inside out and forms a bulb of active sperm, which the female can store in her spermatheca, a pouch within the oviducal gland. The females of some octopus species can store the sperm for up to 10 months! When she is ready to lay her eggs, the female uses this sperm to fertilise them as each one is laid. *Octopus cyanea* can produce hundreds of spermatophores and over several hours will transfer many to the female. Other octopuses, like the giant Pacific octopus, produce only one metre-long spermatophore at a time.

The nature of their cryptic lifestyle makes octopuses asocial. Given their short lifespan (2-3 years) it is natural that when a mature male and female meet, they should start mating without much display or courtship behaviour. These are not times to be choosy about one's sexual partner. The male usually has no one around to fight with for mating rights and females take the opportunity to obtain sperm when they can. Both males and females will mate with multiple partners. One would expect the female to lay the eggs as soon as copulation is over. Any delay increases the risk of falling victim to a predator and not passing her genes on to the next generation. So why does an inseminated female take the extra risk of mating with more males, instead of laying her eggs straight away? She may not yet be fully mature or she may encounter a 'better' male than previous suitors. The selection criteria she uses to evaluate each potential partner are not well understood. The long mating process suggests that the new male may use the spoon-like ending of his special arm to clear the oviducts of any previously placed sperm. Naturally, he wants to transfer his own genetic information to the newborn.

At some point, the female, who may store spermatophores in the spermatheca for as long as two thirds of her lifetime, goes inside her burrow to lay her eggs. It is not known what stimulates egg-laying. As the eggs pass through the oviducal gland, the spermatophores discharge the sperm with a complex mechanically or osmotically activated mechanism. Thousands of fertilised eggs are deposited on the roof of the burrow and hang like grapes. The female will not eat during the three-week incubation period that is typical for tropical species. Instead, she will stay inside the lair to protect, groom and ventilate the eggs using her siphon. The female *Octopus cyanea* can lay up to 600,000 eggs, which hatch into tiny, poorly developed young only 2mm long. They swim up into the plankton and are carried in ocean currents between the coral reefs of the tropical Indian and Pacific Oceans. The starved and exhausted female dies soon after the young hatch and is consumed by starfishes and other scavengers. At about the same age as the female, the male dies of 'old age'.

Mating in decapods, cuttlefish and squid has its own peculiarities. Like all social animals, decapods engage in agonistic (competitive) courtship behaviour. In *Sepia latimanus*, display contests between males are characterised by the spectacular intense zebra display, whereby the animal, using his chromatophores, assumes a zebra-like

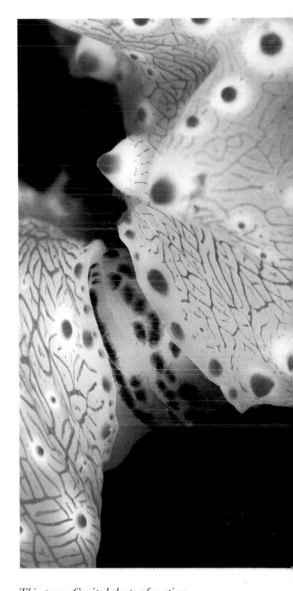

This page: Genital ducts of mating nudibranchs, Halgerda batangas (5cm).

Opposite: Mating nudibranchs, Nembrotha purpureolineata (6cm).

Previous page: Octopus cyanea (40cm) mating. The male is on the right hand side of the picture.

colour pattern. The contest may escalate into physical violence, after which the dominant male acquires mating rights and begins courting the female.

During copulation, the hectocotylised arm, often the first left arm in decapods, acquires the spermatophores one by one with the ligula and deposits them in the spermatheca. In contrast to octopuses, the female *Sepia latimanus* will not store the spermatophores for an extended period, but will go over a coral head to lay the eggs; she will then be ready to mate again. A significant behavioural difference from the solitary octopods is that the male broadclub cuttlefish will temporarily guard the inseminated female, driving away other suitors who want to replace his spermatophores with their own. The female uses her arms to lay the eggs deep among the hard coral branches to protect them from predators. Other than that, there is no parental care for the young that will hatch.

Swimming crabs derive their name from their flattened paddle-like fifth or last pair of legs, which enables them to swim or burrow under the sand or mud. As with most higher forms of animals, decapods are dioecious, i.e. they have separate sexes. Internal fertilisation of the female takes place when the abdomens of the mating pair touch each other as in the photo opposite. The female carries the eggs on the underside of her abdomen. After hatching, the larvae join the planktonic soup where they undergo a series of changes. Once the metamorphosis is complete, those that have survived the planktonic stage settle on the reef.

Nudibranchs are simultaneous hermaphrodites. Their primary sex gland is called ovotestis (ovary and testis). It enables each member of the mating pair to produce both sperm and eggs simultaneously. However, there is no self-fertilisation. When two conspecifics locate each other chemically, you can see them getting more and more excited as the courtship progresses. Because the genital aperture is located on the right side of nudibranchs, the courtship culminates with the animals juxtaposing their right sides so that their genital ducts can meet. Copulation is reciprocal, i.e. both animals function as males, exchanging spermatophores, which are stored in a receptacle known as a spermatheca. As with their octopus relatives, nudibranch fertilisation and laying of eggs are independent of copulation.

Several days later, when the eggs in the ovotestis are fully developed, each nudibranch will seek an appropriate spot – normally a favourite food such as a sponge – in which to deposit an egg mass (see photo p. 146). Nudibranchs acquire their colour from the food they eat, so laying the eggs in a chromatically compatible environment gives them camouflage protection. In some species, the egg mass is quite different in colour. Usually, these are bright colours, warning that the eggs are toxic. The eggs are fertilised as they pass through the spermatheca. They are enveloped by a protective mucus, which holds them together in a long spiral ribbon containing thousands of eggs. Upon incubation, the veliger larvae, characterised by a shell, join the planktonic soup and drift with the oceanic surface currents for anything from a few days up to several months. The larval stage can be prolonged until the free-swimming veliger contacts a shallow reef surface. The larval shell of the veliger is lost during its subsequent metamorphosis into a juvenile nudibranch. Metamorphosis can be delayed if a proper feeding surface is not encountered.

The majority of fishes lay eggs, using one of two types of reproductive behaviour. They either release their eggs in the water column (for example, parrotfishes and wrasses), which is called broadcast spawning, or they lay them on a nest in the substrate (damselfishes, triggerfishes). In the first case, the pair swims together high up in the water column. At the peak of their ascent, the female releases an egg raft. Simultaneously, the male releases the spermatozoa, thus fertilising the eggs.

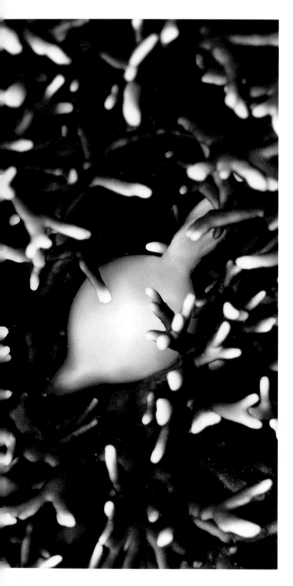

Broadclub cuttlefish egg, Sepia latimanus, among hard coral.

Swimming crabs, Charybdis sp., mating. The male is underneath.

Saddleback anemonefish, Amphiprion polymnus, egg detail. The eggs were photographed two days before hatching.

The reason for swimming towards the surface is that the pair want to lay their eggs as far away as possible from the bottom and its associated predators. The eggs are positively buoyant and they will disperse with the surface currents, maximising their chances of survival. The longer the duration of the pelagic larval stage, the greater the geographic dispersal. This pelagic larval stage ends when the young fish settle on the bottom after encountering a suitable environment such as a shallow reef. During the subsequent metamorphosis, they acquire their juvenile characteristics. Some species are able to prolong their pelagic larval stage until they encounter a suitable shallow reef.

For obvious reasons, fishes that broadcast spawn produce significantly more eggs than those that make a nest. In this second case, the male builds the nest and fertilises the eggs as they are being laid by the female. He then guards them until they hatch. Nesting larvae stay very near the site and settle quickly, whereas the pelagic larvae of broadcast spawners can drift for months and miles. Here are two examples of the two types of reproductive behaviour.

Like all damselfishes (*Pomacentridae*), clownfishes lay their eggs in a nest. The dominant male clownfish gets very excited as the spawning day approaches. He is bold, hyperactive and aggressive, chasing and nipping his mate. During courtship displays, he extends his pelvic, dorsal and anal fins to increase his size, in case his beloved has any second thoughts about whether or not he is the dominant male in the clownfish social hierarchy. The male selects a nest site, usually a rock, next to the host anemone. He spends a lot of time cleaning the site meticulously, removing debris or algae with his mouth. Eventually, the female decides to give him a hand. When the site is ready, she swims slowly over the nest, brushing the surface with her ventral area. If you observe carefully, you will notice her tiny conical ovipositor, which deposits the eggs during each spawning pass. The male swims in the female's wake, fertilising the eggs as they are being laid. This is not an easy task and requires good co-ordination. However, the pair will have plenty of opportunity to practise. Given the limits of their world and their rigid social structure, clownfish pairs have every incentive to stick together. Practice makes perfect and as the pair matures it may produce over a thousand eggs.

Amphiprion eggs, like those in the picture opposite, are about 3-4mm long. They are attached to the nest's surface by a tuft of short threads. The male spends his days guarding the eggs with particular vigilance. He is aggressive towards predators, such as wrasses, which consider the eggs an irresistible delicacy. Simultaneously, he monitors the health of the eggs like a Japanese gardener. Using his mouth, he removes every little speck of debris and clears the nest of dead eggs. He uses his pectoral fins to ventilate the eggs, much as the octopus does with its siphon. The incubation period is made to fit a typical seven-day diving holiday, giving visitors the chance to observe the development of the embryos, which, as the days go by, become more and more visible. When they hatch, the larvae swim to the surface, joining the planktonic soup and drifting with the currents.

The larval phase is short, only about ten days, and this accounts for the localised distribution of many species. A good example is *Anemone City* at Ras Mohammed in the Red Sea. Those of you who have dived this site must have noticed the high concentration of anemones and clownfish in a certain area. The larval stage terminates when the young fish settle on the bottom and go through metamorphosis to acquire their juvenile colours. Metamorphosis is rapid and short, lasting only about a day or so, and each juvenile clownfish must find an anemone quickly, otherwise it will be consumed by a predator. We are unsure as to how various clownfish species locate their

This page: Saddleback anemonefish, Amphiprion polymnus, eggs on coconut.

Overleaf: Juvenile false clown anemonefish (approx. 1.5cm), Amphiprion ocellaris, on Heteractis magnifica. The juvenile was skittish and extremely mobile. Taking this unusual photograph was very challenging.

This page: Painted frogfish mating pair, Antennarius pictus (10cm). The larger fish on the left is the female.

Opposite top: Snail, cf. Casmaria erinaceus, laying an egg mass. This column of eggs is not typical of all gastropods, just the species of the family Cassidae.

Opposite middle: Nudibranch laying an egg ribbon, Hypselodoris maritania (3cm).

Opposite bottom: Mating snails, Pleuroploca trapezium (14cm).

host. There is evidence that some species locate the chemicals released by an anemone and follow the trail to its source. If the resident group of clownfish allows the newcomer to settle, he goes through the acclimation process described earlier. It is worth mentioning that triggerfishes also build nests. Divers should never approach a nest, since the triggerfish is bound to react with ferocious aggression to protect its eggs. The bites will be severe, particularly if they come from the titan triggerfish, *Balistoides viridescens* (see photos p. 51-52).

Frogfishes are solitary animals that do not tolerate each other's presence. In fact, aquarium owners must be particularly careful, since cannibalism has been well documented in aquarium conditions. The only time that frogfish tolerate each other is during reproduction. The big frogfish in the photo on page 145 is the female – her abdomen is enormously swollen by the eggs she is carrying. The male maintains physical contact with her by nibbling her or touching her with his pectoral fin. Her dorsal fins are erect and this is not because she is stressed by the photographer's presence. This, together with a vigorous body undulation (tremor), is a signal to the male of the approaching spawning. From time to time, he will nudge her with his snout, trying to make her swim towards the surface and release the eggs so that he can fertilise them. Until that moment, he has every interest in staying close to the female and making sure that he, and not some other male, is there in the right place at the right time. After mating, the pair separates. If you have frogfish fever, there is only one prescription: a) read *Frogfishes of the World* by Pietsch & Grobecker and *Reef Fishes, volume 1* by Scott Michael, and b) visit Lembeh Strait, the Frogfish Capital of the World.

Not all frogfishes spawn. The male of *Lophiocharon trisignatus* carries the fertilised eggs on the side of his body! The eggs attach to the skin by a double-stranded thread-like structure and form an egg cluster. They are much bigger and significantly less numerous than eggs of other species that result from spawning. Another significant difference is that there is no pelagic larval stage. The eggs hatch directly into miniature adults. The lack of a dispersal larval stage accounts for the narrow geographical distribution of this species. Theodore W. Pietsch and David B. Grobecker speculate that 'this mode of egg carrying has evolved under a dual selective pressure to protect the offspring, on the one hand, and to enhance luring, on the other'. In other words, given the way frogfish camouflage themselves, a fish that attempts to eat the egg cluster on the 'sponge' will find itself in the 'sponge's' mouth.

Some fish families show an unusual variation on nest reproductive behaviour. Cardinalfishes (*Apogonidae*) and jawfishes (*Opistognathidae*) are among the few marine fishes to incubate their eggs inside the male's mouth. In pipefishes (*Sygnathidae*), the male incubates the eggs on the ventral surface near the tail. Some species also have various degrees of brood pouch development.

This page: Cephalopod eggs.

*Opposite: Nudibranch, Nembrotha purpureolineata
(6cm) laying its egg ribbon on an ascidian,
Polycarpa aurata (10cm).*

SEX CHANGE

Sex change is a commonplace occurrence in the underwater world. Various fishes, for example wrasses, parrotfishes, groupers and basslets, live their lives as females, thus maximising the procreation capabilities of their species. However, if conditions demand it, i.e. if the dominant male dies, they are able to undergo a complete sex change. This is known as protogynous (Gr: first female) hermaphrodism and *Pseudanthias squamipinnis* (see photo p. 27) is the classic example. Anthias live in harems with a dominant purplish male and several orange females. When the male dies, the largest female changes her sex and replaces the deceased as a fully functioning male. The opposite change – from male to female – is protandrous (Gr: first male) hermaphrodism, of which the best examples are clownfishes and the ribbon eel. As mentioned earlier, clownfishes live in highly structured matriarchal societies. If the dominant female dies, her male partner undergoes a sex reversal and replaces her. Simultaneously, the second in rank, i.e. the largest of the non-breeding clownfish, becomes the new functioning male. The dominant male has testes and non-functioning ovaries. When sex reversal is stimulated, the testes cease to function and degenerate, whereas the ovaries become active. Sex reversal is essential for the propagation of clownfishes. Otherwise, the dominant male would have either to wait for a female to arrive by chance or to abandon the safety of the anemone and seek a mate, thus facing a high predation risk.

Generally, in clownfishes, there is no colour difference between the sexes. In contrast, the ribbon eel's colouration varies according to its sexual phase. There is some confusion in the literature regarding the sex of each colour phase. The information that follows is based on L. Fishelson, Randall et al. and S. Michael (see References, p. 253-254). The juvenile is black with a yellow dorsal fin. Upon reaching 65-80cm, the transformation into a male begins and the result is a blue ribbon eel with yellow dorsal fin, snout and lower jaw. The female transformation phase starts when the male reaches approximately 85cm. Females are entirely yellow and are rarely seen.

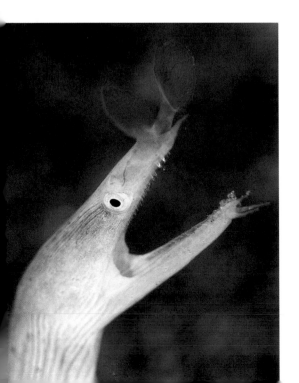

Ribbon eel, Rhinomuraena quaesita (130cm). The black is the juvenile phase, the blue is the male and the yellow is the female phase. The third picture from the top of this page shows a ribbon eel undergoing a sex change from male to female.

RADIAL SYMMETRY AND REGENERATION

Sea stars are characterised by radial symmetry. Five to 20 arms radiate from the central disk and contain duplicate sets of internal organs. As a result, the whole animal can grow from a small fragment. A sea star under attack is able to autotomise (self-mutilate) an arm in order to escape from a predator such as the harlequin shrimp, *Hymenocera picta*. The lost arm is subsequently regenerated. In at least one species, there is asexual replication, whereby an arm will detach itself from the body in order to regenerate and grow into a new animal. Regenerating starfish are easily recognised by their asymmetrical appearance. Since starfish are bottom feeders, their mouth is located on the underside (oral side) and the anus on the top (aboral side) of the animal. This anatomy is shared by sea urchins, which belong to the same family, *Echinodermata*. Sexes are separate. During synchronised spawning, enormous quantities of eggs and sperm are released from the female's and the male's anus like white ash from an erupting volcano. Very few of the free-swimming larvae survive.

Like starfishes, sea cucumbers (also *Echinodermata*) are radially symmetrical and can regenerate missing parts. Some sea cucumber species even exhibit asexual reproduction whereby the body splits in half. The two halves regenerate the missing parts and the process repeats itself. Michael Aw mentions sporadic accounts that Japanese fishermen catch such sea cucumber species, cut them in half and throw the pieces back into the sea to regenerate. In this way they attempt to 'revive' numbers of a fishery under heavy commercial pressure. I have found no documentation to confirm whether this practice is widespread and whether it can revive declining stocks. Besides, this fishery also targets holothurian species that do not reproduce by asexual replication.

Above: Sea star, Fromia monilis (12cm).

This page top: A new starfish regenerates from a detached arm. Notice that the new sea star will have six arms instead of five.

Overleaf: Crinoid shrimp, Periclimenes commensalis (1.8cm).

CRINOID COMMUNITY

Crinoidea (Gr: lily-like) date back 600 million years and thrived during the Palaeozoic period. Today, although quite complex, they show little change in their ancestral characteristics. There are two groups. Stalked crinoids (called sea lilies) are fixed to the substrate by a stalk and cannot relocate themselves. You are likely to see them only if you make a deep dive with a research submersible. There are 80 species living at depths of over 100m. The crinoids (feather stars) that you see during your dives account for 550 species.

The body consists of a central disk. On the underside are the cirri, tubular legs that enable the crinoid to anchor or relocate itself. On the upper side are the branching, feathery arms in multiples of five (from five to 200 arms). Each arm is flanked by two rows of numerous feather-like branches called pinnules. These in turn are flanked by thin hair called podia, which have a mucous coat. An ambulacral groove runs down the centre of each arm. The pinnules function as a fishing net, capturing plankton with their mucus. The plankton runs down the ambulacral groove with the help of invisible tiny hairs – cilia – which direct the food towards the crinoid's mouth. Remember that in other echinoids, sea urchins and sea stars, the mouth is located on the underside (oral side), since the animals are bottom feeders. Because crinoids filter their food from the water, the mouth is located on the upper side. The anus is also on the upper side, situated on an elevated cone.

Crinoids use their cirri to climb on top of sponges or gorgonians in order to gain maximum exposure to the nutrient-rich current. They can fan out their arms using a series of joints. Primarily nocturnal, they take advantage of the fact that, at night, plankton rises from the depths, increasing the concentration of nutrients near the surface. Crinoids are abundant on the reef and do not seem to have any predators. Like their close relatives, the sea cucumbers, they may have skin toxins that serve as a predator deterrent. In fact, their bright colours may act as a warning of their toxic substances (aposematic colouration). It is not surprising that crinoids should attract commensal guests, since they can provide free food and board. Shrimps, squat lobsters, clingfishes and worms are favoured residents. They move up and down the ambulacral groove, intercepting small quantities of food, and it is possible that they may supplement their diet with crinoid mucus. The effect on the crinoid is infinitesimal. It is extremely difficult to locate these commensal animals because of their size and excellent camouflage. A number of fishes, particularly juveniles, seek temporary protection among crinoid arms. However, they do not use the crinoid's food supply.

I have always wondered how crinoid shrimps can match the colour of their host. Here is the answer. Crinoid shrimps settle on their host after the end of their larval stage, then slowly adopt colours that match those of the crinoid. Like cephalopods, crustaceans have chromatophore cells. Each such cell is highly branched and contains a combination of one or several colour granules, yellow, orange, red, brown and black. To change its colour, the crustacean must simply change the colour distribution in the chromatophores. This process is controlled by hormones produced by the so-called X-organ, which is located in the eyestalks, and stored inside the sinus gland, which in turn regulates the amount and circulation of those hormones in the bloodstream. Herein lies the big difference between crustaceans and cephalopods. Both have chromatophore cells, but cephalopods can change colour instantly, because their chromatophores are controlled by the nervous system. In contrast, crustaceans change their colour over time, because their chromatophores are under hormonal control.

This page: Feather star worm (0.7cm), crawling on a crinoid arm.

Opposite: Crinoid or feather star, Crinoidea. It is worth mentioning that crinoids do have one enemy: divers with bad buoyancy control. It is most embarrassing to emerge from a dive with crinoids attached to one's wetsuit like velcro. My understanding is that the crinoids do not like it either.

This page: Crinoid clingfish, Discotrema sp. (3cm). These clingfish were impossible to photograph during the day because the crinoid's arms were furled. I returned to the same location at night when the host's arms stretched out to feed, exposing the clingfish.

Opposite: Female squat lobster, Allogalathea elegans (2cm). There was also a male on the same crinoid, distinguished by his smaller size. But he was always seen hiding among the crinoid's cirri and was impossible to photograph.

This page: Crinoid shrimp, Periclimenes cornutus (1.5cm).

Opposite: Crinoid shrimp, Periclimenes commensalis (1.8cm).

Overleaf: Dendronotid nudibranch, Melibe fimbriata (20cm). This nudibranch resembles a mass of algae. It has large cerata with a rounded oral hood around its mouth. It predates upon crustaceans, which it traps using its oral hood. Additional nutrition is derived from symbiotic zooxanthellae. Most Melibe species can swim by moving their body from side to side.

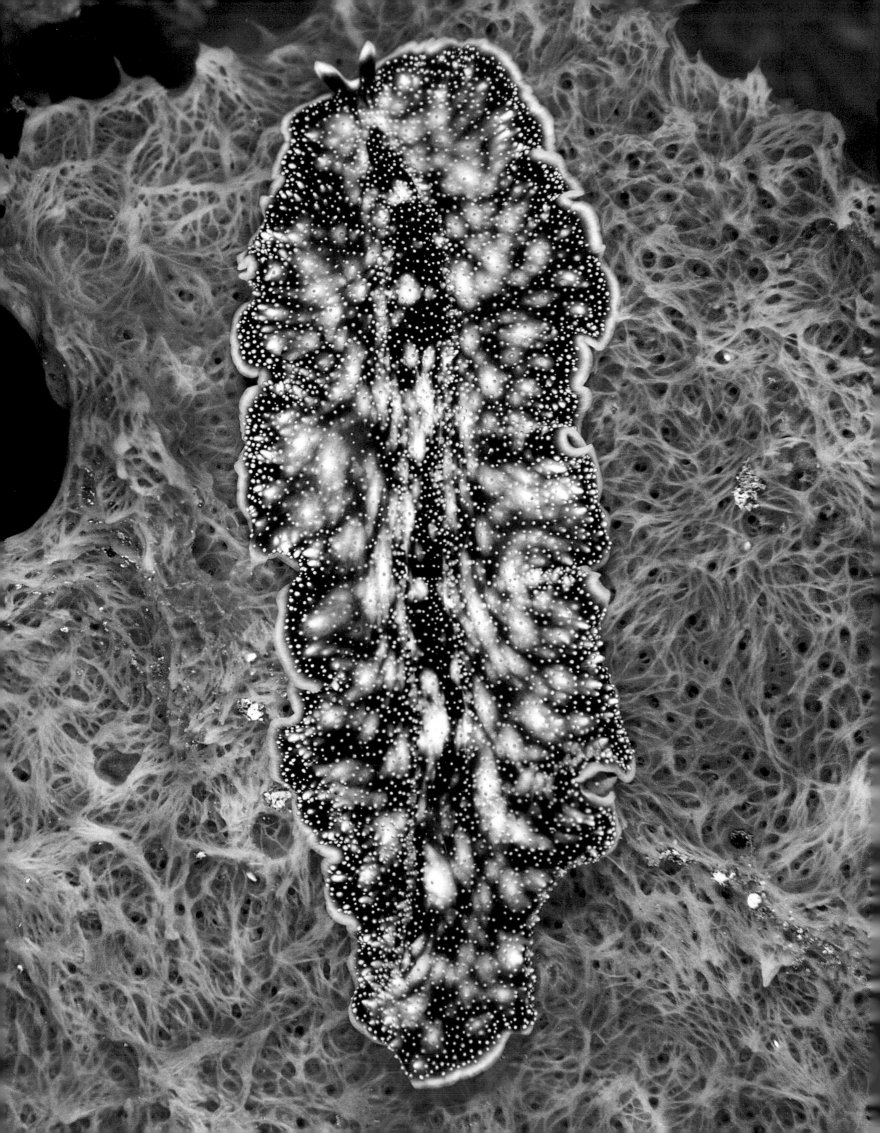

Snails & Nudibranchs

Did you know that cephalopods and nudibranchs belong to the same phylum (Mollusca)? Yes, although it might seem surprising, they are both molluscs. Molluscs are divided into three classes: Gastropoda (Gr: stomach foot), Bivalvia (L: two valved) and Cephalopoda (Gr: head foot). Gastropods are further divided into one terrestrial and two marine subclasses: Pulmonata (L: lung), Prosobranchia (Gr: anterior gill) and Opisthobranchia (Gr: posterior gill). Divers are fascinated by snails (Prosobranchia) and sea slugs (Opisthobranchia), which include the fantastic nudibranchs. For land snails and slugs (Pulmonata), you must forsake diving and go on a land excursion. Sacrilege!

Snails live a secretive lifestyle during the day to avoid exposing themselves to predators such as triggerfishes. Most use their muscular foot to bury themselves under the sand. They come out at night to feed and you will see them at various dive sites, including the KBR house reef, *Hairball*, *Aer Parang* and *Goby-A-Crab*. Of course, there are nocturnal predators that can either smash their shell (mantis shrimps) or drill holes into it (spined murex snails, octopuses). Snails crawl using their muscular foot, which secretes mucus that reduces friction. When in danger, the foot is retracted inside the shell and in some species the aperture is sealed with a solid trapdoor known as the operculum. The shells are made of calcium carbonate secreted by the snail's mantle. In cowries, the mantle temporarily envelops the shell's outer surface and gives it a brilliant lustre. Do not be tempted to touch the exposed mantle, as you are likely to damage it, particularly if you wear gloves.

Tridacna clams (see photo p. 177) are under severe fishing pressure from humans and are rare in many places. They are listed in Appendix II of CITES (the Convention on International Trade in Endangered Species). A species is listed in Appendix II when it may be threatened with extinction unless international commercial trade is not regulated. Trade is not prohibited, but is monitored under a permit system. I thought that the size and weight of the *Tridacna gigas* shell would oblige free divers to spare the clam. However, they cut and remove the adductor muscle with a knife, thus collecting the prized meat without having to bring the large shell to the surface. Obviously, this makes the lives of poachers much easier. Mariculture seems to be the way to meet the growing demand. However, in a report published in 1995 by TRAFFIC International, the wildlife trade monitoring programme of WWF (World Wide Fund for Nature) and IUCN (World Conservation Union), Glenn Sant mentions that his personal observations indicate the possibility of the laundering of wild stocks, which are sold with mariculture-produced giant clams.

This page: Egg Cowry, Pseudosimnia marginata (1.8cm).

Opposite: Flatworm, Thysanozoon nigropapillosum (12cm). Unlike nudibranchs (L: naked gills) that breathe through their feathery gills, flatworms absorb their oxygen requirements through their flat body surface.

This page: Dorid nudibranch, Halgerda batangas (5cm) laying an egg ribbon.
Opposite top: Sea slug, Philinopsis cyanea (4.5cm).
Opposite middle: Chromodorid nudibranch, Chromodoris leopardus (6cm).
Opposite bottom: A rare species of conch, Strombus thersites (15cm).

This page: Chromodorid nudibranch, Ceratosoma trilobatum (10cm).
Opposite: Moon snail, Naticarius orientalis (2cm).

Bivalves, as the name implies, consist of two separate halves held together by strong muscles. Some bivalves attach themselves permanently to the substrate, whether rock or coral. The most famous of these bivalves is the giant giant clam. In the Lembeh Strait, impressive giant giant clams can be seen at *Lettus Surpriz U* (see photo p. 177).

Bivalves are filter feeders. Water reaches the gill chamber through a pair of openings in the mantle. Nutrients are withheld by gill mucus and transferred to the mouth. Other bivalve species bury themselves under the sand during the day and emerge at night to filter feed. Octopuses prey on them by drilling holes into their shell. The objective is to drill the hole where the muscle that attaches the animal to the shell is located. What is remarkable is that the octopus does not drill holes at random. Although the location of musculo-skeletal attachment varies among shell types, the octopus drills the hole precisely over the site of muscle attachment. The digestive enzymes of the saliva loosen the muscle and thus separate the animal from the shell, enabling the octopus to gain access to it.

Unlike other gastropods, the evolutionary trend in sea slugs (opisthobranchs) has been towards the reduction or complete loss of the shell. Bubble shells (*Cephalaspidea*) have lagged behind in this process and a few species possess a conspicuous, fully functional shell (see photo p. 173). Others have only the remnants of a shell, either vestigial or internal. Bubble shells are the most primitive and numerous of the opisthobranch species. It should be noted that most opisthobranchs, including nudibranchs, have a shell during their larval stage. Except for *Cephalaspidea* and some *Anaspidea*, the shell is lost during metamorphosis.

Nudibranchs (L: naked gills) are definitely the prima donnas of the reef. There is a profusion of nudibranchs in the Lembeh Strait. On every dive you can easily spot ten or more different species. Molluscs are such a diverse group that it is impossible to generalise on particular features. The same is true of the nudibranchs. I will describe the two main groups, dorids and aeolids. Complete descriptions of the various other groups can be found in invertebrate identification books (see References, p. 253-254).

Dorids (*Doridacea*) are the largest nudibranch group. They have a pair of tentacles (rhinophores) on top of their head and a gill plume on their lower back. The anus is situated in the middle of the gill plume. In some species, the gills can retract inside a branchial pocket if disturbed. Phyllidiids are a group of dorid nudibranchs that lack dorsal gills. Instead, there is a secondary set of gills along the underside of the body margins. Diet varies among the groups of dorid nudibranchs. The majority feed upon sponges, but in some dorid groups the diet consists of bryozoans, tunicates or other sea slugs.

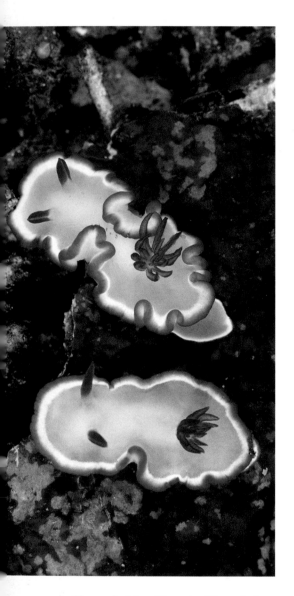

Chromodorid nudibranchs, Glossodoris averni (6cm).

Aeolid nudibranch, Phyllodesmium longicirra (14cm).

This page: Aeolid nudibranch, Flabellina exoptata (3cm).
Opposite top: Phyllidiid nudibranch, Reticulidia halgerda (7cm).
Opposite middle: Side-gilled slug, Euselenops luniceps (7cm).
Opposite bottom: Chromodorid nudibranch, Chromodoris geometrica (2.5cm).

This page: Juvenile egg cowry, Ovula ovum (12cm).
Opposite: Snail, Cymbiola sp.

This page: Bubble shell, Hydatina physis (4cm).
Opposite top: Chromodorid nudibranch, Chromodoris kuniei (5cm).
Opposite middle: Chromodorid nudibranch, Glossodoris cruentus (4.5cm).
Opposite bottom: Phyllidiid nudibranch, Phyllidia ocellata (6cm).
Overleaf: Spanish Dancer, Hexabranchus sanguineus (25cm).

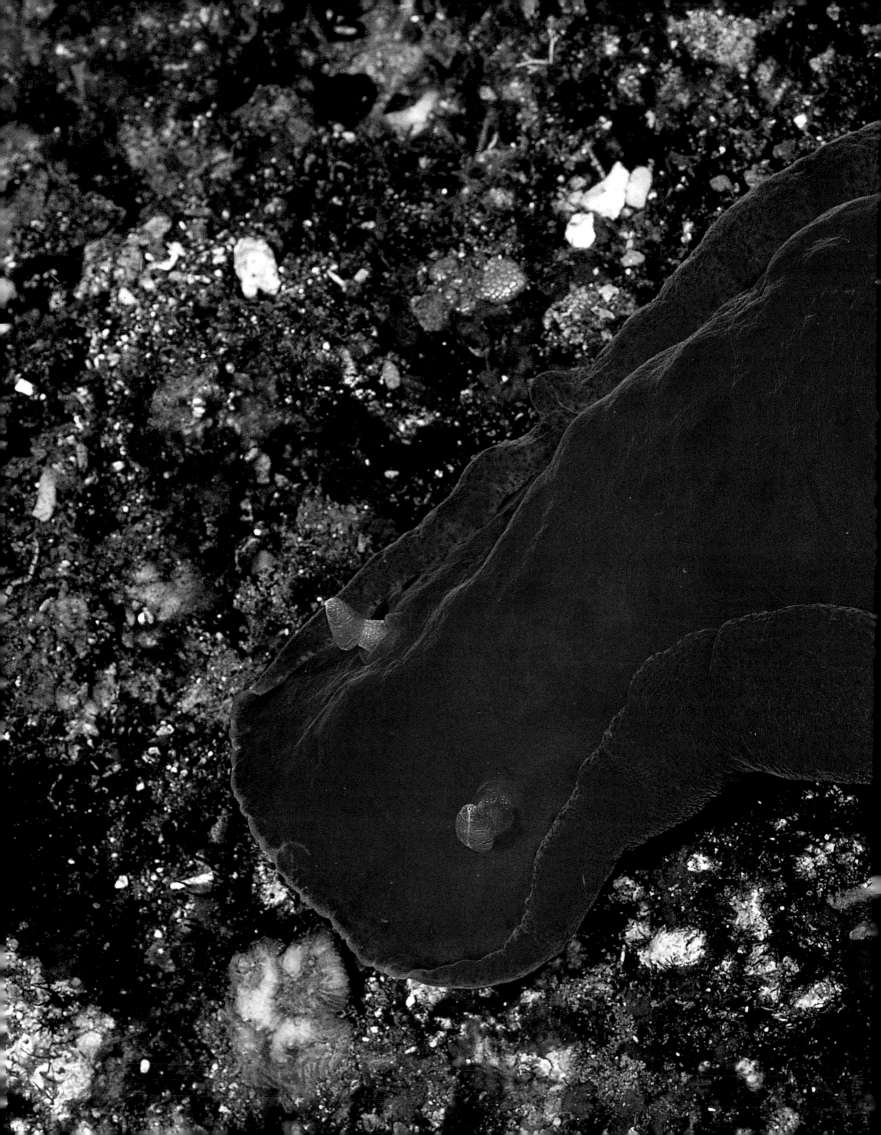

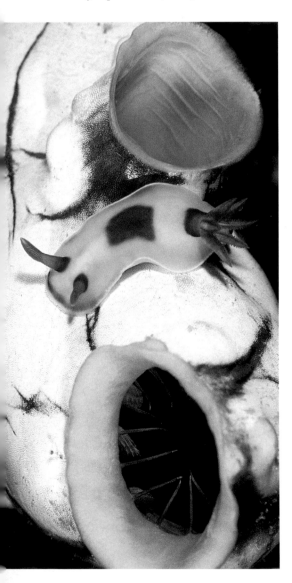

Aeolids (*Aeolidacea*), the second largest nudibranch group, have finger-like dorsal projections called cerata, which contain extensions of the digestive system. A fascinating feature of aeolids is their ability to acquire defences from their food source. They retrieve unfired nematocysts (stinging cells) from their cnidarian prey – hydroids, soft corals, gorgonians, etc – and store them in special sacs at the tips of their cerata. Usually, cerata tips are brightly coloured to warn potential predators about the presence of nematocysts. Incidentally, the tentacle tips of certain sea anemones, such as *Heteractis magnifica* and *Entacmaea quadricolor*, are also brightly coloured to warn of the presence of nematocysts.

In general, nudibranch defences derive from their food source. Some rely on a perfect camouflage that matches the colour of their prey (sponges, seaweed, cnidarians). They acquire their prey's colours through consumption. The majority relies on aposematic colouration, i.e. vibrant colours that advertise their toxic qualities or foul taste. Toxins are acquired through their diet. Looking for nudibranchs on a dive is like trying to find a needle in a haystack, unless you do some homework and learn what they eat. Checking for nudibranchs on algae, sponges, ascidians, bryozoans, and cnidarians is a good way to start.

The rhinophores of nudibranchs are chemosensory. This means that they enable nudibranchs to detect chemicals released by nearby animals, sense their habitat and locate their food or mating partner. Nudibranchs, like snails, feed using a radula, a rather complex tongue-like structure that is equipped with sharp chitinous teeth. During feeding, the radula scrapes tissue from the food item. Any broken teeth are quickly replaced. Some nudibranchs lack radular teeth. Instead, they secrete a digestive enzyme on to their food and then suck the partially digested tissue.

Several nudibranch species still wait to be discovered and classified. Nudibranch identification can be very difficult. Sometimes, external features suffice to determine the genera. Often, the genus can be determined only by specimen examination, to compare similarities or differences in radular teeth.

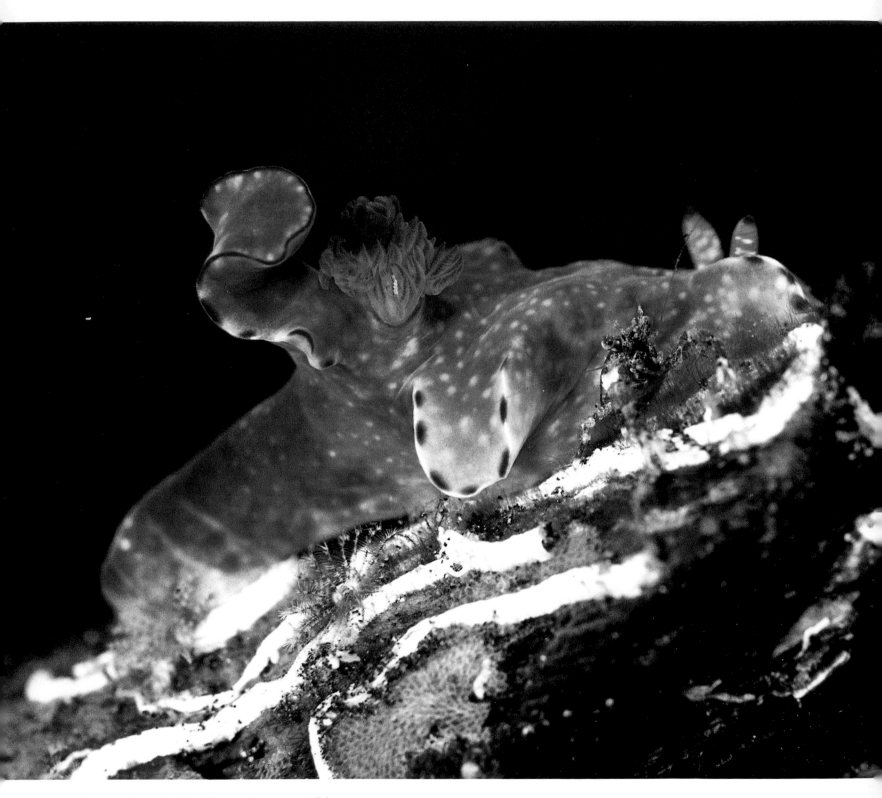

This page: Chromodorid nudibranch, Ceratosoma trilobatum.
Opposite top: Chromodorid nudibranch, Hypselodoris sp.
Opposite middle: Chromodorid nudibranch, Hypselodoris iacula (5cm).
Opposite bottom: Flatworm, Pseudoceros bifurcus (6cm).
Overleaf: Jans's pipefish, Doryrhamphus janssi (13cm).

SEAHORSES & PIPEFISHES

Seahorses, pipefishes and sea dragons belong to the family *Sygnathidae* (Gr: fused jaw). All seahorses belong to a genus whose name is the ancient Greek word *Hippocampus*. Ancient Greeks gave mythical attributes to the seahorse, perceiving it as a sea monster, *campus*, with the head of a horse, *hippos*. Seahorses are teleost (bony) fishes, equipped with fins, gills and a swim bladder. Rings of bony plates cover their body for protection. Their eyes can move independently, like those of a chameleon.

There is considerable confusion regarding seahorse species even among the scientific community. Dr Amanda C. J. Vincent and her colleagues at Project Seahorse undertook the Herculean task of sorting things out. Given their popularity, it is surprising how little we know about seahorses, even regarding their anatomical features. For example, the function of their little anal fin is still unknown.

Seahorses are diurnal and rely on camouflage for survival. They can blend in with their environment by virtue of their ability to change colour and grow skin filaments. Their inconspicuous presence on the reef makes them hard to find. Once a seahorse is located, there is no need to become frantic and try to take the picture or video at all costs. Guides will certainly not allow you to stress the animal and expel it from its microhabitat. Seahorses are territorial and show minimal mobility. They prefer to use their monkey-like tail to stay at one feeding place. They are typical ambush predators, much like frogfishes. They remain motionless, blending with their surroundings and waiting for unsuspecting prey, such as small benthic crustaceans and fish fry. Like frogfishes, seahorses have no teeth. They suck their prey whole with their long tubular snout. A small shrimp disappears in an instant. As there is no stomach, the prey goes directly through the digestive system. Predators include humans, frogfishes, crabs and pelagic fishes.

Seahorses are mostly famous for the fact that it is the male who carries the eggs. Seahorse eggs and sperm are fewer in number than those of other teleost fishes. During courtship, the pair changes colour and starts pivoting while hooked on a common holdfast. Occasionally, they go for a small promenade along the bottom and back to pivoting. Eventually, they will rise to the surface to mate. A great photo opportunity! However, do not forget to check your air gauge while waiting; courtship may last for up to nine hours.

Synchronised movements are very important, since the female must align her ovipositor with the opening of the male's brood pouch so that she can deposit her mature eggs. The eggs are fertilised inside the male's brooding pouch. Just before copulation, only mature eggs are hydrated. The others continue their development until they are ready for the next mating. The female can store hydrated eggs for only about 24 hours. If a mating partner is not found, she will simply discard the mature eggs. Depending on the species and water temperature, the male broods the developing embryos for ten days to six weeks.

Seahorses are born as miniature replicas of their parents (average size 6-12mm). About 1,000 individuals are born in the larger species and as few as one or two in the tiny pygmy seahorse. The juveniles receive no parental care and must survive on their own. In contrast to their parents, they are very vulnerable to predators. The adult pair usually mates again the very same day. The seahorse species that have been studied so far appear to be monogamous. Both partners ignore any other suitors. In fact, while the male is incubating the eggs, pair bonds are reinforced by ten-minute daily greetings,

Above: Ornate ghost pipefish, Solenostomus paradoxus (12cm).

Opposite: Pygmy seahorse, Hippocampus bargibanti (<2cm).

Below: Pygmy seahorse shown at actual size.

Yellow seahorse, Hippocampus kuda. (17cm). Colour variations are shown opposite.

Thorny seahorse, Hippocampus histrix (13.5cm). This individual was photographed during daytime, at a depth of approximately 30m. It was hovering above the substrate, hunting prey that was invisible to the naked eye. Whenever it came upon anything interesting, it would freeze, stalk the prey and eventually suck it with its long tubular snout.

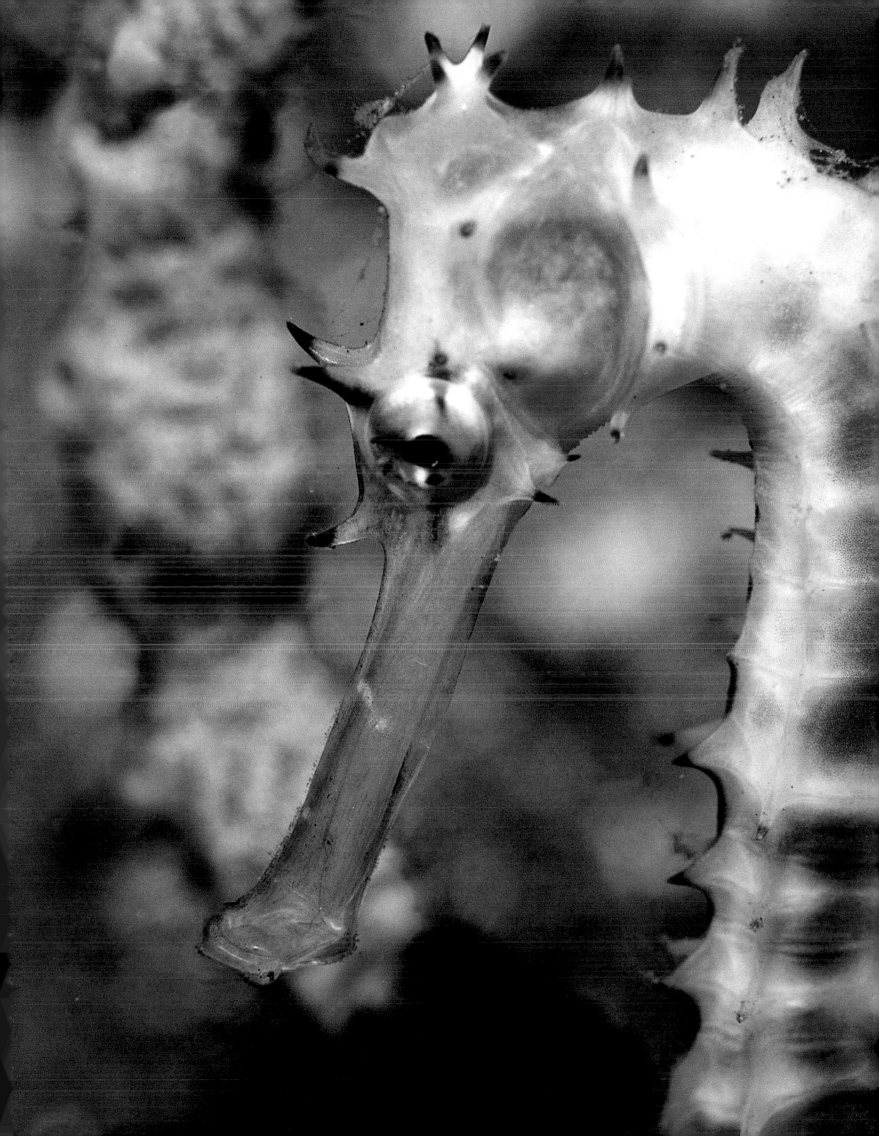

This page: Unidentified seahorse, Hippocampus sp. This species is often confused with Hippocampus minotaur.
As this book went to print, S. A. Lourie & J. E. Randall were working on a scientific paper to describe this species.

Opposite: Juvenile pygmy seahorse, Hippocampus bargibanti (about 1cm). The irregular bulbous tubercles scattered over the body and tail perfectly match the polyp structure of the host gorgonian, Muricella plectana.

Page 190: Ornate ghost pipefish, Solenostomus paradoxus (12cm).

Page 191 top: Robust ghost pipefish, Solenostomus cyanopterus (16cm). The small individual is the male.

Page 191 bottom: Robust ghost pipefish, Solenostomus cyanopterus (16cm).

which are short versions of courtship. Having said 'good morning' to each other, the pair separates for the rest of the day. It seems that these daily greetings are important in order to synchronise the couple's reproductive cycle. In this way, the female will have mature eggs ready so that she can refill the male's pouch as soon as the eggs hatch.

It was Christmas Day and I was the only diver from the resort who had decided not to miss a dive. I had the whole of Lembeh Strait to myself and I wished it were Christmas every day. I chose *Aer Parang* for the first dive. At a depth of 4m, there was a male *Hippocampus kuda* pivoting on a holdfast. His brood pouch was enormous and his movements indicated that the eggs were about to hatch. I was so excited. This was going to be a very special Christmas. Pictures of a seahorse giving birth. That would certainly make the other guests green. The first hour went by and the seahorse was still pivoting. I surfaced, changed tank and went back down. Another hour and still nothing. The seahorse kept pivoting. I rushed back to the resort to find out what was wrong with him. As it turns out, male seahorses pump and thrust for hours before ejecting fully independent young. The next day I went back to the same spot early in the morning. The seahorse was still at the same holdfast, but it was obvious from the size of his pouch that the eggs had hatched.

Ornate ghost pipefishes and robust ghost pipefishes (*Solenostomidae*) are extremely hard to locate since their colour mimics weeds, algae or invertebrates. Ornate ghost pipefishes are often found among crinoids, where they match the colour of the crinoid and are impossible to differentiate from its arms. Robust ghost pipefishes can be seen drifting like seaweed. Ghost pipefishes are usually seen in pairs, of which the male is the smaller. They hover vertically, hunting small crustaceans that they catch by suction using their long snout. Unlike seahorses and pipefishes, it is the female who incubates the eggs in a brood pouch formed by her fused pelvic fins.

The bizarre appearance of the seahorse has attracted our curiosity, admiration and love. Some prefer them as earrings, others as a means to cure impotence. Their destiny seems to be to suffer a slow death drying in the sun. According to global trade data compiled by Project Seahorse, at least 20 million dried seahorses were traded worldwide in 1995, primarily for use in Traditional Chinese Medicine (TCM) and its derivatives. Demand rose greatly in the 1980s as a result of China's economic restructuring and the associated rise in per capita income. Suppliers were unable to meet demand, prices increased and trade expanded globally. Today, seahorses appear to be a lucrative alternative for subsistence fishermen in overpopulated areas, where fishing stocks have been overexploited by the use of destructive fishing techniques (trawling, dynamite and cyanide fishing). Furthermore, we should not forget that seahorses are part of the bycatch of trawlers around the world.

Many divers view TCM with scepticism. It is hard to believe that seahorses help cure a wide range of diseases – asthma, heart disease, broken bones and of course impotence, to name only a few. Moreover, the seahorse is supposed to be an aphrodisiac like tiger parts or rhino horn. How is it possible to accept such claims within our Western culture? Yet, in *Seahorses: An Identification Guide to the World's Species and their Conservation*, Lourie, Vincent and Hall state that TCM, which has been recognised by the World Health Organisation as a valid form of medicine and is accepted by more than one quarter of the world's population, has been formally codified for about 2,000 years and has been using seahorses for the last 600 years. As an individual you are entitled to your own opinion regarding the validity of TCM. However, conservationists should focus their efforts on relieving pressure on seahorses, whatever its cause. As Lourie and her colleagues argue, collaboration, not confrontation, with TCM traders and consumers is the key for addressing the issue of overexploitation and finding sustainable alternatives.

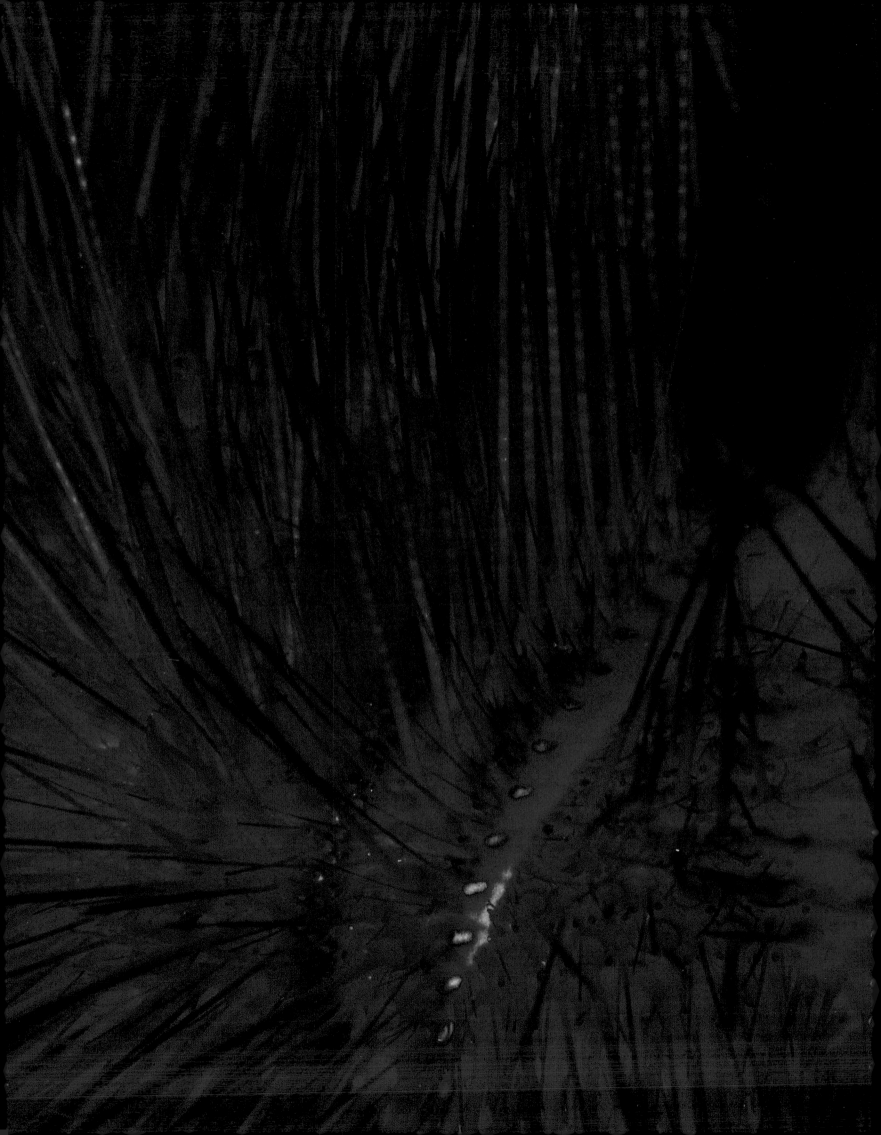

FISHES

Most recreational divers want to see fish. That is not a problem, since the reefs around the world are packed with fish competing for space, shelter and food. Those that have the best survival strategy will procreate and pass their genes to the next generation.

The Lembeh Strait is best known for those fishes that have adopted a benthic (bottom-dwelling) lifestyle. These ambush predators have the most energy-efficient hunting strategy. They remain motionless, often for long periods of time, disguising themselves with camouflage colours which make them virtually invisible to divers and, more importantly, to passing fish.

Their anatomy is adapted to their sedentary lifestyle. They may be quick enough to swallow passing prey, but their bodies are definitely not streamlined for fast swimming. But then this is not an important function for them. Instead, they need to be negatively buoyant in order to cling to the substrate. As a result of their lifestyle, some benthic predators, notably frogfishes, have 'lost' their swim bladder, their equivalent of a buoyancy control device. Does this mean that frogfishes are like sitting ducks for other predators? Certainly not! They protect themselves by imitating a background, such as a sponge, which is uninteresting to potential predators. Some frogfishes may have toxic properties, but this has yet to be adequately documented.

There are three species in the humpback scorpionfish group, *Scorpaenopsis diabola*, *Scorpaenopsis gibbosa* and *Scorpaenopsis macrochir*. The critical feature in distinguishing the three species is the colouration of the medial (inner) side of the pectoral fin. Why would a fish have bright colours in a place where they are not always visible? This is, in fact, an ingenious example of aposematic colouration. The venomous humpback scorpionfish blends perfectly against the background and remains unnoticed. Any vivid colours would simply betray its position. However, once detected by a predator, the scorpionfish must be able to issue a warning about its venomous spines, which is achieved by flaring its pectoral fins to expose their bright colours. The same thing occurs inadvertently when the fish swims from one ambush location to another. Another scorpionfish, the spiny devilfish, *Inimicus didactylus*, uses aposematic colouration in a similar way.

How can benthic predators match the colour of their surroundings so well? Chromatophore cells determine fish colour. These cells are under hormonal and nervous control. Hormones regulate more permanent dramatic colour changes, whereas the nervous system is responsible for instant, less dramatic variations. For example, when a scorpionfish shifts location, the chromatophores receive a stimulus from the nervous system and alter the hues to achieve a better match with the surroundings. In contrast, the hormones of a giant frogfish, *Antennarius commerson*, take several weeks to institute a dramatic colour change from black to orange.

Frogfishes cannot swim like other fish. They use jet propulsion to change living quarters. Water is expelled from the gill apertures located behind the modified pectoral fins (see photo p. 206). These apertures work much like the siphon of the octopus. When the fish settles on the substrate, it uses its leglike pectoral fins to walk and to hold itself in place.

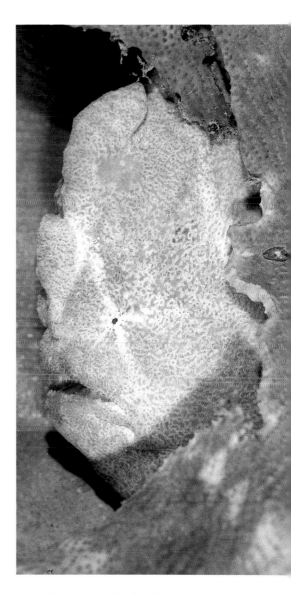

Lembeh Strait is undoubtedly the Frogfish Capital of the World. Frogfish fans will find several spectacular species, such as the two giant frogfish, Antennarius commerson (30cm), pictured in these two pages.

Previous page: Juvenile red emperor, Lutjanus sebae (60cm), seeking refuge among the spines of a fire urchin, Astropyga radiata (20cm).

This page: Striated frogfish, Antennarius striatus (22cm).

Opposite top: Striated frogfish, Antennarius striatus (22cm).

Opposite middle: Striated frogfish, Antennarius striatus (22cm).

Opposite bottom: Ambon scorpionfish, Pteroidichthys amboinensis (8cm).

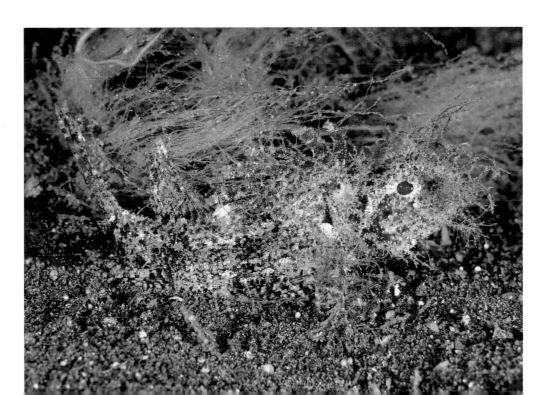

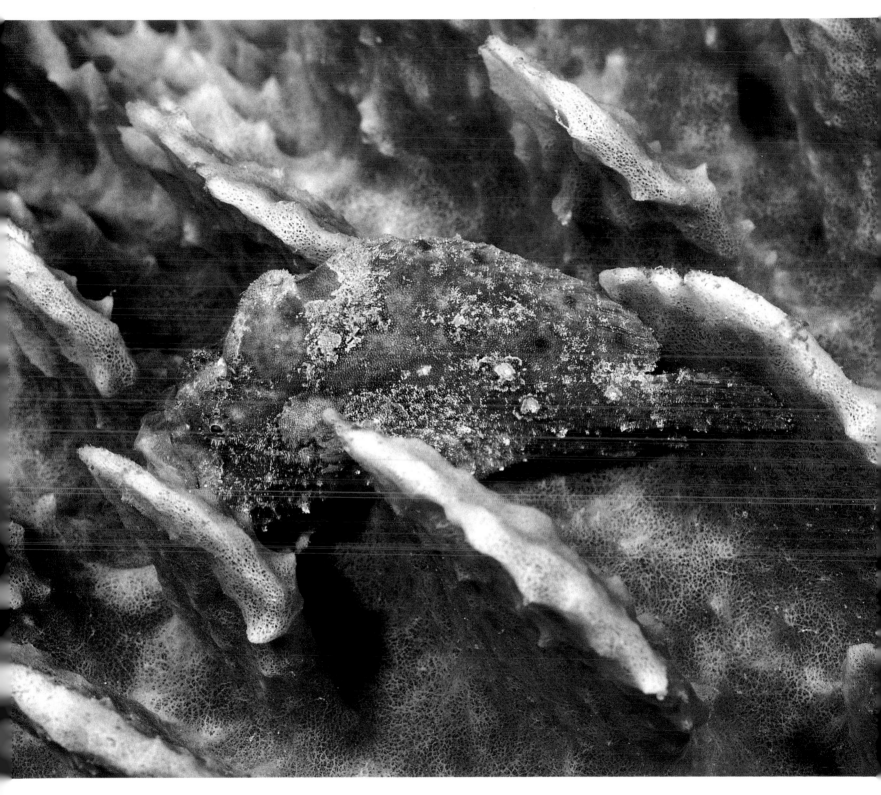

This page: The scarlet frogfish, Antennarius coccineus (13cm), a very cryptic species, blends perfectly with the colour and texture of the barrel sponge, Xestospongia sp.

Opposite top: Painted frogfish, Antennarius pictus (10cm).

Opposite middle: Wartskin frogfish, Antennarius maculatus (10cm).

Opposite bottom: Painted frogfish, Antennarius pictus (10cm).

The Lembeh Strait has so many venomous scorpionfishes that visiting divers are given an excellent incentive to perfect their buoyancy skills before visiting the area. Scorpionfishes are masters of camouflage and an accidental contact with their venomous spines may even cause death. The symptoms of poisoning are similar among the various species, but vary in degree. The reef stonefish, *Synanceia verrucosa*, is the most venomous of all fishes (see photo p. 229). Its dorsal spines are very sharp and can penetrate the sole of a tennis shoe. The venom causes excruciating pain, which may last several days. The victim may lose consciousness and drown or suffer a cardiac arrest. Symptoms include complete paralysis of the injured limb, swelling, delirium, nausea, fever, respiratory distress, convulsions and death. Complete recovery from a severe stonefish sting may require several months, with adverse effects on the victim's general health. The Commonwealth Serum Laboratories in Melbourne, Australia, have developed an effective *Synanceia* antivenin, which can be administered to counteract poisoning by other scorpionfishes as well. Anyone diving in remote locations should keep in mind that availability of the antivenin might be at best problematic. Certified rescue divers should review first-aid procedures before a dive trip. By the way, a first-aid course is of paramount importance for any diver.

Venomous Rock, as I named it, is located at a depth of 9m, just in front of KBR's pier. During a night dive there, I found a reef stonefish with superb camouflage. There were also three big scorpionfish (about 20cm) on the same rock. The very thought that there might be a second stonefish as well, since they are occasionally found in pairs, gave me an eerie feeling and a strong incentive to watch my buoyancy. I checked the rock over and over again, and although I did not see a second stonefish, I still have my suspicions. Despite persistent attempts, I was unable to locate the stonefish during the daytime, though for the duration of my stay it was always seen at the same spot at night.

Stonefishes are scaleless, like moray eels. The latter secrete copious amounts of slime to protect their skin from parasites. Stonefishes use another parasite-protection method. Their skin produces a cuticle, a protective membrane that covers their body. Stonefishes regularly shed the encrusted cuticle to relieve themselves from parasites and other encrusting organisms, such as algae, bacteria and hydroids, which grow on their skin due to their benthic lifestyle. If the parasitic infection is severe, the cuticle is shed more often. Some reef stonefish turn vivid pink after shedding their cuticle. *Rhinopias* and other scorpionfishes also shed their cuticle.

Spiny devilfish, Inimicus didactylus (18cm), in three colour variations. The muck dive sites of Lembeh Strait are littered with the venomous spiny devilfish. Divers who kneel on the sand to take a picture should think twice. The devilfish often buries itself under the sand during the day to ambush passing fish. The unusual red colour variant can be seen at Critter Hunt, particularly at night, when the devilfish emerge to hunt. The rubble substrate of this dive site is full of reds and the devilfish matches the surroundings superbly. Divers should be extremely cautious regarding their buoyancy.

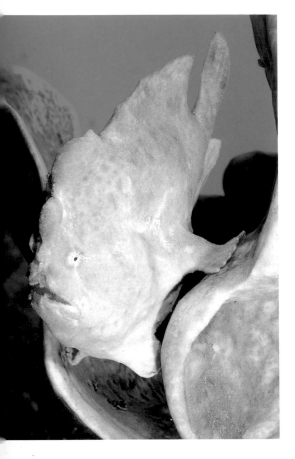

In addition to their superb camouflage colours, stonefishes enhance their camouflage with algae. These plants may also act as a passive lure to bring herbivorous fishes, such as parrotfishes or butterflyfishes, within striking distance. The stonefish opens its mouth, expanding its cavity dramatically. This creates a vacuum, and prey is drawn in by the resulting suction. The stonefish shuts its mouth. The whole enterprise lasts approximately 15 milliseconds.

Frogfishes, which use the same technique, are even faster. The jaws project outward in 6 milliseconds, while the mouth cavity expands twelvefold. This is probably the fastest strike in nature. There is a resident yellow frogfish at *Angel's Window*. It just sits there on the reef wall, swallowing butterflyfishes one by one. The human eye cannot trace the feeding action. Simply count the butterflyfishes in the vicinity from time to time and you will be able to deduce the casualties. Similarly, because of the lightning speed, the butterflyfishes remain unaware of the predation taking place and blissfully continue their grazing.

Frogfishes or anglerfishes use a 'fishing rod' to attract a wide range of prey, which can be surprisingly oversized. The rod is the elongated first dorsal spine (illicium), whose fleshy tip (esca) acts as bait. Depending on the species, the esca may look like a worm, shrimp, amphipod or small fish. The rod is usually laid back on the head. When prey swims nearby, the frogfish uses this fishing apparatus to attract its attention and bring it within striking distance. Bringing the illicium forward, with a technique reminiscent of fly-fishing, it exposes the bait to the prey. The lure's movements vary, depending on whether the esca resembles a worm or a fish. If the prey succeeds in biting the lure, the frogfish can regenerate the esca fully within four to eight months. In his *Historia Animalium* (ca. 344 BC), Aristotle was the first to give a remarkably accurate description of the way anglerfishes use their lure. His account was based on observations of the common Mediterranean anglerfish species, *Lophius budegassa* and/or *Lophius piscatorius*.

The strike zone of lie-in-wait predators such as frogfishes or stonefishes becomes a prime ungrazed foraging site. This is only natural, since any fish that comes within range is devoured. As a result, marine plants are allowed to grow undisturbed. The lush vegetation of this ungrazed strike zone becomes a tempting meal for herbivorous fishes that fail to recognise the inconspicuous predator. As they come to graze, they are devoured, and so the cycle continues.

Space on the reef is at a premium. Every small patch seems to be occupied by one creature or another. As a result, the empty area around an ambush predator seems like a perfect shelter site. Remember the reef stonefish at *Venomous Rock* in front of the resort? After a dusk dive, I decided to visit my lethal friend and observe him. Moments later, a butterflyfish came and settled on the nice little crevice created between the stonefish's body and the rock. I immediately covered my light so as not to interfere with the action. The butterflyfish had settled for the night in death's embrace. The stonefish made an imperceptible movement to improve its striking angle and waited. The prey, however, remained closer to the stonefish's tail. It was a great behavioural shot, but I was so intrigued to see what would happen that I simply forgot to lift my camera. Eventually, the butterflyfish escaped by sheer chance. Obviously, the reason this stonefish was at the exact same location on *Venomous Rock* every night was that the fish seeking shelter provided a continuous food supply.

Top: Giant frogfish, Antennarius commerson (30cm). A detail of its gill aperture is shown above.

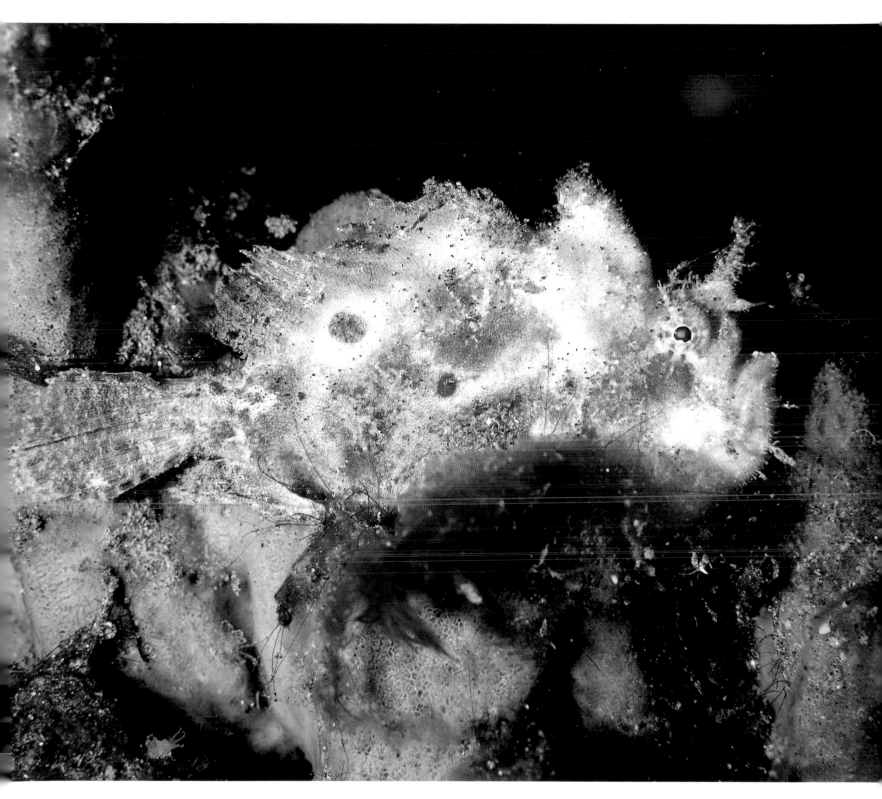

Coinbearing frogfish, Antennarius nummifer (13cm).

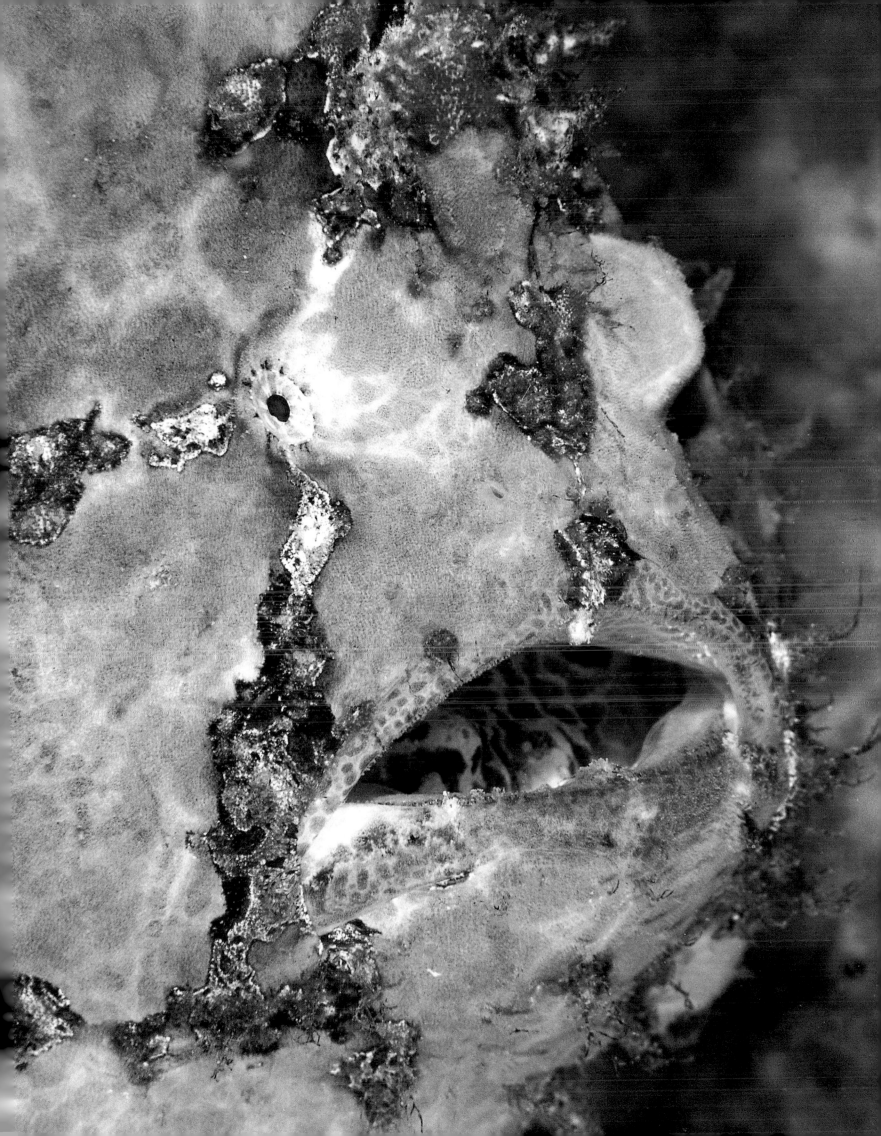

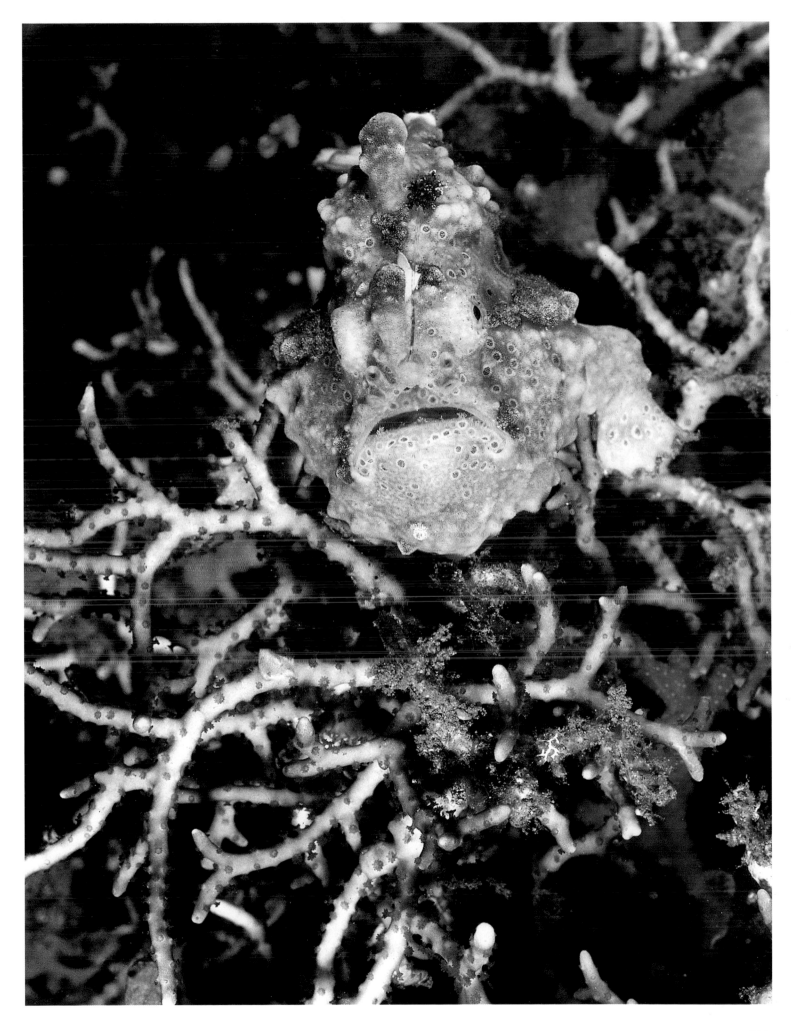

There is an interesting frogfish story associated with the photograph on the opposite page. While doing my advance dive planning, I decided with Wilson to do a night dive in front of the KBR pier and check the small sponges that are scattered along the rubble slope leading into the Lembeh channel. I took a six-hour surface interval, since I wanted to explore the deeper end of the slope. We dove at slack tide. At about 20m, Wilson spotted a small sponge which had turned into an incredible microhabitat. There was a sharpnose puffer, *Canthigaster compressa*, resting for the night. But what attracted our attention were a tiny pink frogfish (about 3cm) and a platoon of squat lobsters. The frogfish was gorgeous. However, the squat lobsters were unwilling to share their habitat with a stranger. They kept pinching the frogfish, which constantly shifted position in an effort to escape. The squat lobsters were so many that they were not willing to surrender an inch of their precious space. They just would not let the frogfish settle anywhere on the sponge. We were witnessing one of the many usually unseen or unnoticed battles for space on the reef. Unfortunately, my dive computer started complaining and we had to ascend. I was so excited that I volunteered to guide any KBR guests who wanted to see and photograph this gorgeous fish. The next day we waited until the strong current subsided and went to the same spot. The frogfish was gone. Presumably it had eventually been driven away by the squat lobsters, probably taking a ride on the current and settling somewhere else.

Lionfishes use their enlarged pectoral fins to corner their prey (crustaceans, small fishes and cephalopods) against the reef. The pectoral fins act as a fan or net that blocks all escape routes. At dusk, their colour is dull, due to the low light levels, and their stripes serve as disruptive camouflage, to confuse their prey. In broad daylight, their bright colours are a warning to potential predators. However, their poisonous spines are not a sufficient deterrent for certain resolute carnivores, such as frogfishes. The latter will not even hesitate to prey on the ferocious mantis shrimp. Lionfishes can inflict a painful sting which, in rare cases, can be fatal.

The ambon scorpionfish, *Pteroidichthys amboinensis*, develops dermal appendages in order to match its surroundings better. Not all the ambon scorpionfish that you will see in the Lembeh Strait have long filaments on their skin. You will find them in those individuals that live in algal environments. The striated frogfish, *Antennarius striatus*, is another example of filamentous ornamentation.

Rhinopias are undoubtedly the kings of scorpionfishes and they are extremely rare. 'Please find me a *Rhinopias*,' photographers begged the KBR dive guides. The task is daunting even for a seasoned guide, since *Rhinopias* have a cryptic lifestyle and excellent camouflage. In addition, their habitat is often outside the range of the typical dive site. Only three *Rhinopias* have ever been spotted in the Lembeh Strait. Two of those were seen during my stay. The news about the presence of this rare fish immediately travelled on the web, and some divers came specifically to photograph it.

Here is the *Rhinopias* saga. The dive guides spotted the purple and the red *Rhinopias* at *Angel's Window*, at approximately 40m, on the rarely visited rubble slope. The red *Rhinopias* appears 'bright red' only because of the photographer's flash; at this depth, due to refraction and colour absorption, it looked brown, much like the small sponges that lay on the rubble substrate. *Rhinopias* are also known to rock backwards and forwards, mimicking a piece of debris. Because this was a deep dive, we hovered in midwater, trying to spot the fishes before descending deeper. Although we knew their whereabouts, we had difficulty distinguishing the two *Rhinopias* from the substrate. In addition, they were surprisingly mobile. During most dives, they were between 35 and 40m. I made a chart with the depth sightings and it was apparent that the fishes had a tendency to move deeper. In fact, quite often the red *Rhinopias* could not be seen and

Page 208: Juvenile wartskin frogfish, Antennarius maculatus (10cm).

Page 209: Giant frogfish, Antennarius commerson (30cm).

Page 210: Raggy scorpionfish, Scorpaenopsis venosa (22cm), photographed at night on a pillar of the KBR pier.

Page 211: Wartskin frogfish, Antennarius maculatus (10cm).

Opposite: A small sponge on a seemingly barren rubble slope becomes a fascinating microhabitat. There is a juvenile frogfish, Antennarius sp., with a sharpnose puffer, Canthigaster compressa (9cm), hiding behind the sponge. Numerous squat lobsters were pinching the frogfish in an attempt to evict the tiny intruder from their precious sponge habitat.

This page: Weedy scorpionfish, Rhinopias cf. argolida (15cm). Note the strongly rounded and not incised dorsal fin, as opposed to the more incised one seen on the Rhinopias frondosa on page 217.

Opposite top: Longspine waspfish, Paracentropogon longispinis (12cm).

Opposite middle: Blue-eyed stingfish, Minous trachycephalus (10cm).

Opposite bottom: Longspine waspfish, Paracentropogon longispinis (12cm).

was probably below 40m. Some guests wanted to try a deeper dive to locate the rare fish, but the resort refused to grant such dangerous requests. This is a wise but not an easy decision since, at times, resorts may come under pressure to satisfy their clients.

I was tempted to visit the spectacular fish every time there was a dive at *Angel's Window*. However, I believe that 'hot' creatures often receive unnecessary stress from over-eager divers and are eventually driven away. I did only two dives to secure my shots and thereafter relied on other guests to record the depth sightings in my logbook. On January 27 1999 the two *Rhinopias* disappeared and passed into the realm of legend.

The pair of white leaf fish on page 220 were inside a small cave-like crevice at *Angel's Window*, where the prime fishing location is a piece of sponge branching into the middle of the crevice. The leaf fish used this spot to ambush small fishes that regularly used the crevice as a refuge during the day. It was obvious that whoever was on that sponge had more access to food. On two separate occasions, the other individual swam to the sponge to claim this prime ambush site. The first time, I was so excited that I missed the shot. In both cases, the leaf fish did not stay together for long. I was concentrating on the photo and did not take notice of the specifics of this behaviour. One individual was smaller, probably the male. It would have been interesting to note which of the two individuals had access to this desirable feeding site and how many times the site was challenged successfully by the other fish. But, after all, I am a photographer and not a marine biologist.

Taxonomists disagree as to whether waspfishes belong in the family *Scorpaenidae* or have their own separate family, *Tetrarogidae*. They are benthic predators. The cockatoo waspfish (see photos p. 26, 224) looks like so much algal debris found on the seabed and mimics it by swaying from side to side with the surge. Its perfect mimicry confuses divers, prey and fish-eating predators alike. The dorsal spines of waspfishes are highly venomous. Their sting is extremely painful and can be lethal.

Reef fishes swim around in rainbow colours. Divers are perplexed by their bright colours and even scientists seem confused. According to T.M. Gosliner and D.W. Behrens, 'In contrast to terrestrial organisms, our knowledge about the role and importance of colouration in marine organisms is in its infancy.'

For pelagic fishes, such as certain sharks or tuna, the counter-shaded colour pattern, light ventral and dark dorsal area, is simple to understand. When looked at from above, their dark back blends with the dark blue water, whereas from below their light belly matches the bright sunlit sky. In this way, they blend perfectly with the monochromatic blue water background.

This page: Ambon scorpionfish, Pteroidichthys amboinensis (8cm).

Opposite: Yellow coral goby, Gobiodon okinawae (3.5cm), on crown-of-thorns starfish, Acanthaster planci (50cm).

Page 216 top: Wheeler's shrimp goby, Amblyeleotris wheeleri (8cm).

Page 216 middle: Yellownose shrimp goby, Stonogobiops xanthorhinica (5.5cm), hovering to feed on the nutrients brought by the current.

Page 216 bottom: Sailfin shrimp goby, Amblyeleotris randalli (11cm).

Page 217: Weedy scorpionfish, Rhinopias frondosa (23cm).

Leaf fish or leaf scorpionfish, Taenianotus triacanthus (10cm). Leaf fish are not usually seen so close together, however in this case they were contesting a prime ambush site.

Leaf fish or leaf scorpionfish, Taenianotus triacanthus (10cm).

This page: Comet, Calloplesiops altivelis (16cm).

Opposite: Mimic filefish, Paraluteres prionurus (10cm), and soft coral Siphonogorgia cf. godeffroyi. As its name suggests, this filefish mimics the small poisonous pufferfish Canthigaster valentini (9cm). It feeds on coral polyps.

Cockatoo waspfish, Ablabys taenianotus (15cm).

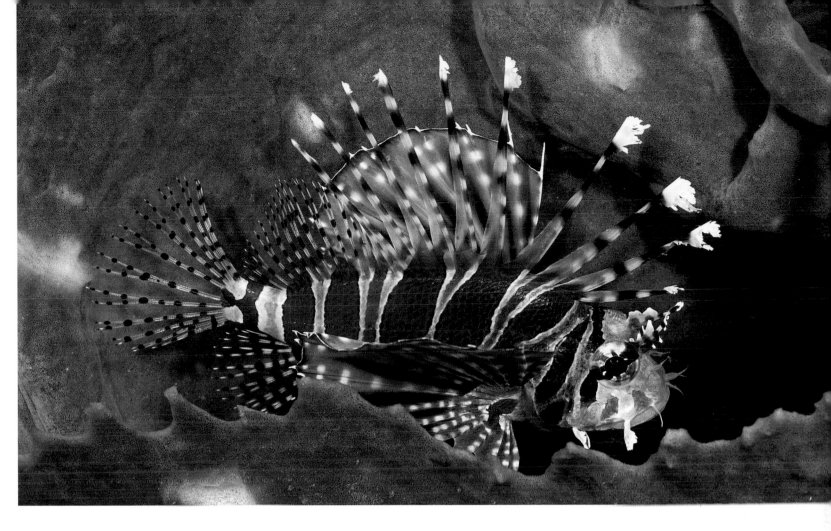

Top: *Zebra lionfish, Dendrochirus zebra (18cm).*

Bottom: *Serrate or pygmy lionfish, Brachypterois serrulata. This scorpionfish was known from specimens trawled from depths between 23 and 79 metres. Roger Steene was the first person to photograph it using scuba. He found it on a sandy slope south of the port city of Bitung in the Lembeh Strait. The pygmy lionfish is also encountered in Secret Bay in Bali where it is also rare. In fact I know of one photographer who has been trying to photograph it for the last four years. I saw the fish ten minutes into my second dive in Secret Bay where this shot was taken.*

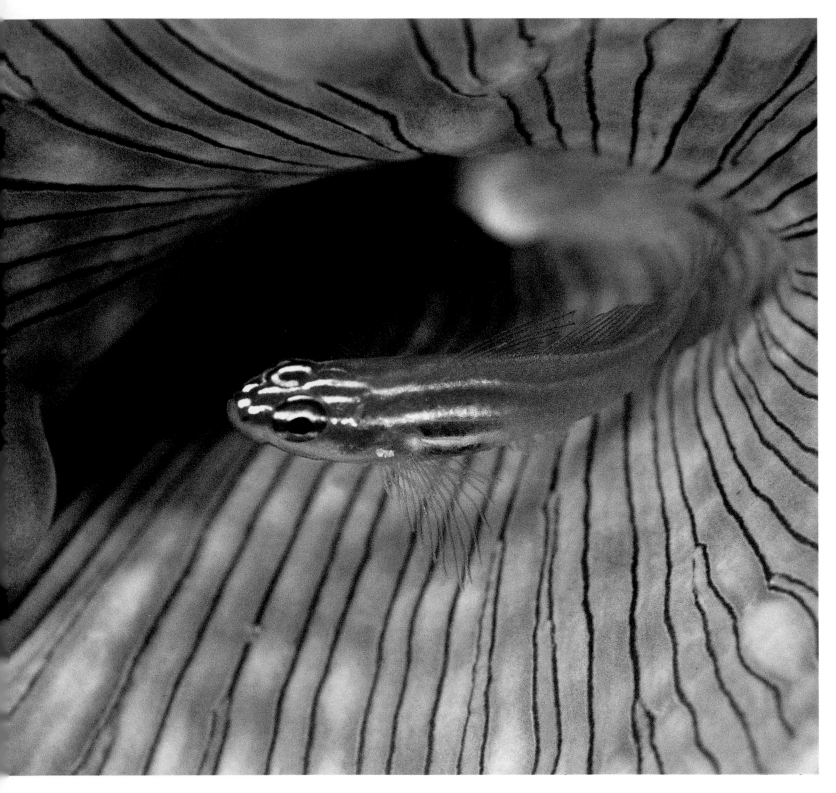

This page: Neon pygmy goby, Eviota pellucida (2.8cm).
Opposite: A yellow blenny, Ecsenius sp., using a barrel sponge to play hide-and-seek with the photographer.

What about reef fishes, then? Why are they so colourful? Why do they risk advertising their presence to potential predators? Do they use bright colours to find a suitable conspecific with which to mate? The theories vary and it is precarious to generalise. Some fishes may use aposematic colouration to warn potential predators about toxins. For example, mandarin fish, *Synchiropus splendidus*, produce a toxic body slime and their bright colours may serve as a warning of their distasteful properties. Some fishes may use cryptic or disruptive colouration, stripes, bars and spots, to break up their shape. However, it is a fact that many fishes, such as butterflyfishes and angelfishes, exhibit vibrant colours that make them stand out against the background. At first glance it may seem that the bright colours of many diurnal reef fishes expose them to predators, but colour may be an irrelevant factor in the predation process, since many fish-eaters – barracudas, jacks, cuttlefishes, etc – are relatively inactive during the day, when colourful reef fishes forage around the reef. They hunt at dawn or dusk and in these low-light situations colours simply do not show. Predator eye anatomy shows that they have poor colour vision and excellent low-light vision. Therefore, it seems more likely that they rely on shape and movement, not colour, to track their prey.

In contrast, the eye anatomy of diurnal reef fishes suggests that colour vision is important for them. This leads to a prevalent theory that good colour vision and colour are important factors for the reproduction of reef fishes. Bright colours may serve for identifying a conspecific and for courtship. This may also be the answer as to why there is such a dramatic colour change between the juvenile and adult stages of certain fishes: it may serve to distinguish mature adults from immature individuals and thus facilitate the mating process. Of course, juveniles face a high risk of predation. Some may use their distinct colours to conceal themselves from potential predators or to signal that they are not a threat to mature conspecifics guarding a territory.

Today, even the popular 'false eye' theory is being challenged. Some fishes have a false eye, the ocellus, near the base of their tail and a dark bar covering the true eye. Theoretically, this would confuse the predator, who would attack the tail thinking that it was the head. However, this speculation should be viewed in light of the fact that daytime predation is minimal. In fact, ambush predators, such as frogfishes, appear to be the only daytime risk. In this case, false eyes are of no significance, since frogfishes and scorpionfishes use suction to engulf the whole victim and do not go for the head-like tail. Critics of the false eye theory argue that if masked and false eyes were a successful survival tool, then these colour markings would have been adopted by the majority of reef fishes through the eons of evolutionary process. In fact, some fishes seem to ignore this full-proof protection. Their eyes are not only not masked, but they are very conspicuous. The function of these markings seems to be intraspecific recognition. If you want to explore the colour dilemma more, read Wilson and Wilson's *Pisces Guide to Watching Fishes: Understanding Coral Reef Fish Behaviour* and Scott Michael's *Reef Fishes, volume 1* (see References, p. 254).

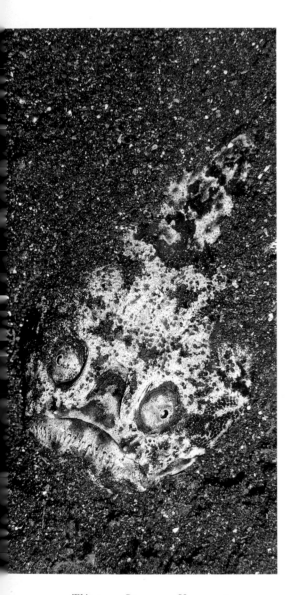

This page: Stargazer, Uranoscopus sulphureus (35cm).

Opposite: Reef stonefish, Synanceia verrucosa (35cm), photographed at Venomous Rock.

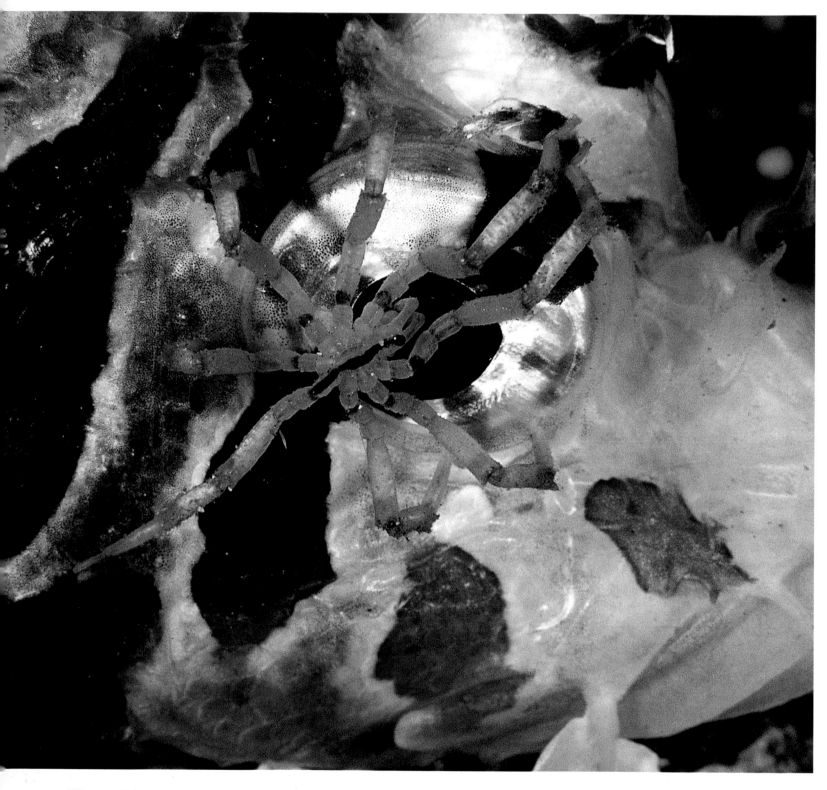

This page: Zebra lionfish, Dendrochirus zebra (18cm). This picture was taken at the end of a night dive in front of the KBR pier. I noticed the sea spider walking over the body of the lionfish, 'killed' my light and waited. Eventually, the sea spider walked over the eye and descended to the rubble bottom to continue its rounds. Pycnogonids or sea spiders form their own group of arthropods. They have 4-6 legs. Males usually carry the eggs.

Opposite: Black comb-toothed blenny, Ecsenius namiyei (7cm). Notice the minuscule mantis shrimp on top of the eye.

Above: Scribbled pufferfish, Arothron mappa (60cm). Notice that the puffer is defecating. Some scientists suggested that I should have collected the excrement, left, for analysis. Personally, I prefer to take photos.

Opposite: Jawfish, Opistognathus sp. (12cm).

Female Morrison's dragonet, Synchiropus morrisoni (7cm). According to Dr Ronald Fricke,
'This represents a new record of the species from Indonesia, which is however not too surprising as the
species is known from Ryukyu Islands and southern Japan and widely extends on the Pacific Plate.'

Juvenile brown tang, Zebrasoma scopas (20cm).

Crab-eyed gobies, Signigobius biocellatus (6.5cm).

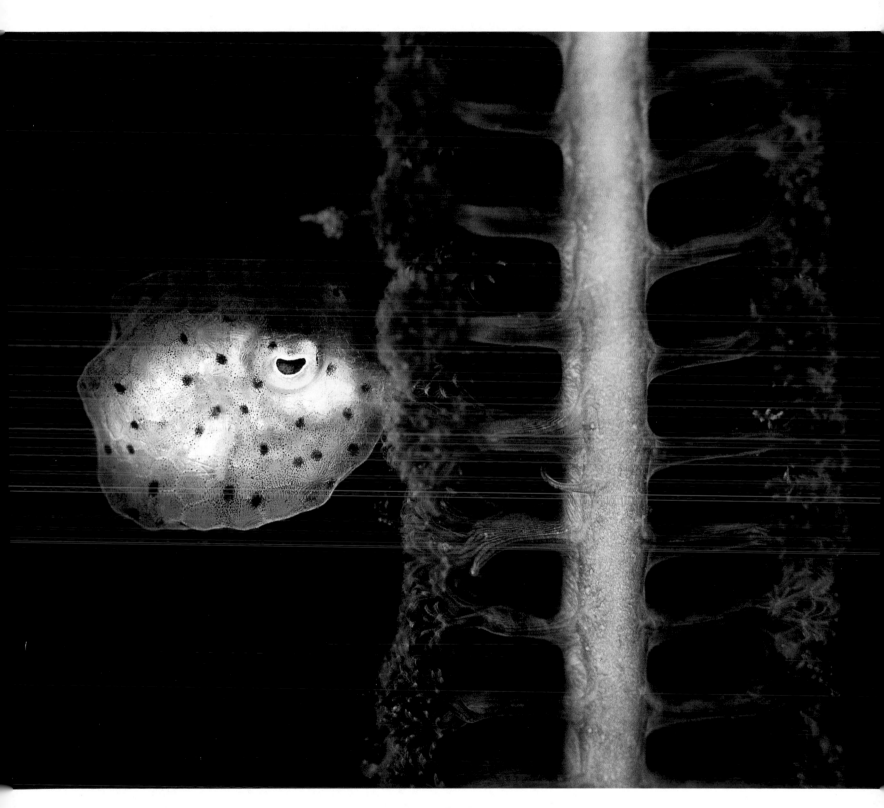

This page: Juvenile longhorn cowfish, Lactoria cornuta (46cm). This fish was less than 2cm.
Overleaf: Leaf fish or leaf scorpionfish, Taenianotus triacanthus (10cm).

EPILOGUE

The Lembeh Strait Preservation Society has been fighting to have the Lembeh Strait declared a marine park. Silvester Benny Pratasik volunteered to conduct a field survey, prepare the relevant proposal documenting the unique biodiversity of the area and submit it to the authorities. I had the privilege of diving with him and assisting him in his efforts. By that time, I was a seasoned Lembeh diver and I wanted to impress Benny by showing him my secret spots and my weird-looking friends. However, to my surprise, he seemed not to be very interested in the various fishes that I was pointing out. After a while I understood that it was only out of politeness that he took any notice at all. He was primarily interested in those low life forms that nobody pays any attention to. He became particularly excited, not over the ambon scorpionfish, but at discovering an unusual sea squirt species. In fact, it was the incredible biodiversity of sessile invertebrates that impressed him.

I took several photos per his suggestions so that he could document this biodiversity in his report. I was proud to assist him, and at the same time learned to view every inhabitant of the reef as an important link in the whole ecosystem. After all, did you know that sea squirts, also called ascidians or tunicates, belong to the same phylum, Chordata, as *Homo sapiens*? Yes, the lowly sea squirts are our nearest invertebrate relatives. Their larvae have a rudimentary backbone, which disappears as they develop into adults. Adult sea squirts are filter feeders, using two siphons. Water enters through the mouth, the largest siphon, food particles are trapped in a net-like filter and the water is expelled through the second and smaller siphon. In this way, sea squirts can filter up to 200 litres of water per hour.

In concluding, I feel that I must address the issue of global warming. The signs are all around us and we can no longer afford the luxury of looking the other way and pretending that everything is as usual. Here are some disturbing figures quoted from the highly recommended *No-Nonsense Guide to Climate Change* by Dinyar Godrej.

'Today's carbon dioxide levels are 30 per cent above pre-industrial levels. The ice sheet that covers the Arctic Ocean has lost 40% of its volume over the last 30 years...[The] forecasts [predict] an almost 40 centimetres rise in sea waters by 2080 if nothing is done about greenhouse gas emissions.'

For the Maldives, the threat from the rising sea water level is real. It is happening today and not at some debatable forecasted future date. In fact, the government is already spending $13,000 per metre of coast to protect the shorelines.

This page: Ascidian, Polycarpa aurata (10cm).

Opposite: Orange cup coral polyps, Tubastraea sp. This is an ahermatypic coral colony. Since they do not have algae in their tissues, ahermatypes are not dependent on sunlight. As a result, they can colonise dark places, such as caves or overhangs, where hermatypes cannot grow. The polyps are voracious carnivores, extending their tentacles mostly at night to capture zooplankton.

To reverse the global warming trend, it would be nice to have carbon sinks to remove the excess carbon dioxide from the atmosphere. A few more forests would help but half the world's original forest cover has been destroyed over the last 40 years. Between 1995 and 1997, the forest area destroyed in Brazil was twice the size of Belgium.

What about coral reefs, our other major carbon sink? In 1998, the hottest year on record since temperature records began, bleaching affected most of the tropical coral reefs resulting in thousands of square miles of graveyard coral. Although this is bad news for the dive industry, the problem is far more serious than a few unhappy divers. Since coral reefs are a major sink for carbon dioxide, binding it to form limestone, they are an integral part to the planet's ecosystem. With our two major carbon sinks - forests and coral reefs - in peril, we are orchestrating our own demise.

The Kyoto climate conference in 1997 was a step in the right direction. At last world leader's recognised the problem and were willing to meet to discuss ways to reduce emissions of greenhouse gasses. However, national interest and the preservation of the status quo overshadowed what is good for the planet. Industrialised nations, representing 20% of the world's population and producing 90% of the greenhouse gases, wanted to find ways to address the problem while maintaining the current lifestyle of their constituents. Developing countries, on the other hand, wanted to exercise their right to pollute in order to expand economic development and offer their citizens a higher standard of living.

As this book goes to print, the Kyoto protocol is being challenged and so is our future. But because books ought to end with a positive note, let us look the other way and talk about diving.

The photosynthesis-dependent coral reef as we know it ends at 150m, where light can no longer reach and photosynthesis ceases. This is the edge of the coral reef and the start of the abyss. The 60-150m frontier territory is often referred to as the 'twilight zone'. This area has been off-limits to divers using scuba, and scientists have had to rely mostly on trawling methods. The popularisation and development of rebreathers and mixed gas diving are opening new frontiers for scientists and divers alike. The future seems exciting and promises to reveal many new fishes and other marine animals.

This page: Phyllidia varicosa (7cm) on an ascidian, Polycarpa aurata (10cm).

Opposite: Nudibranch, Chromodoris strigata (4.5cm) and tunicates.

Page 244: Shrimpfish, Aeoliscus strigatus (14cm).

Page 247: Crinoid shrimp, Periclimenes cornutus (1.5cm).

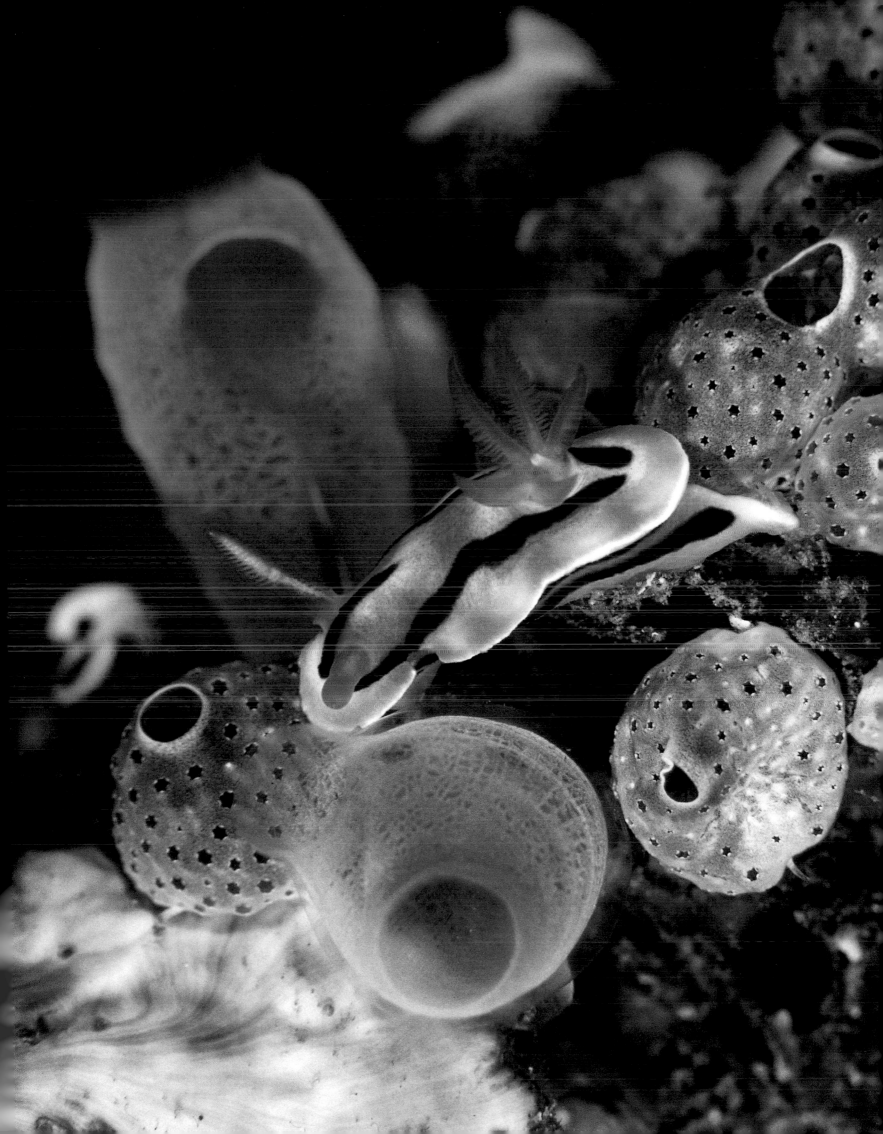

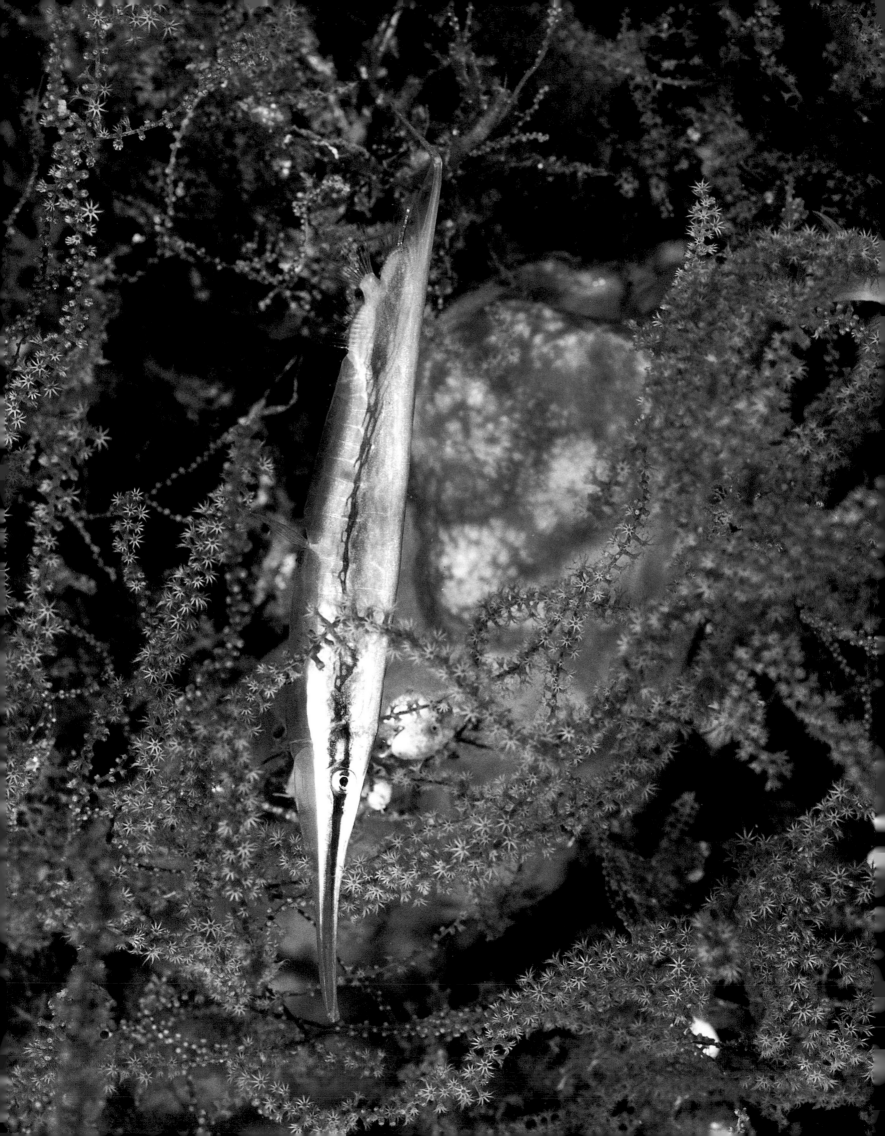

Ahermatypic asymbiont corals: These are the corals that for the most part do not have symbiotic algae (zooxanthellae) in the cells of their polyps. Therefore, unlike hermatypic corals (see below), they do not require sunlight, since they do not depend on algal photosynthesis for their nutrition. As a result, they are not restricted to shallow sunlit waters and can grow at any depth. Divers can observe asymbionts, such as the orange cup corals (*Tubastraea*, *Dendrophyllia* and *Balanophyllia*), by examining overhangs, where the lack of light prevents the growth of hermatypes. In this way, by hiding away from the sun, ahermatypes avoid being displaced by the faster growing reef-building corals. Ahermatypic corals are carnivorous. Like sea anemones, they feed by extending their polyps and paralysing their prey with their stinging cells. Their diet consists primarily of plankton. Note that there are asymbiont corals that secrete calcareous skeletons and so do contribute slowly to reef building.

Aladin Air-X: A dive computer that, among other things, informs the diver about the depth, duration of the dive and remaining time, to avoid decompression sickness. It should be noted that all dive computers, irrespective of brand, are based on decompression models and that none can guarantee absolute safety, particularly concerning repetitive dives over long periods of time. Divers should perform computer-assisted and not computer-controlled diving.

BCD: Buoyancy Control Device. A vest used by divers to regulate their buoyancy by adding or removing air.

Benthic animals: organisms that live on the seafloor. Frogfishes and scorpionfishes are an example of bottom dwellers.

Cyanide fishing: Cyanide divers dilute sodium cyanide tablets into plastic bottles containing water. In Indonesia the resulting chemical solution is called *obat* – literally 'medicine'. When the diver squeezes the bottle, the cyanide solution is ejected and stuns the fish. In this way he can even reach fishes, such as the mandarin fish, that hide in inaccessible coral crevices. Once the prey is stunned, the diver breaks the coral and captures the semi-conscious fish. In the process, and as the cyanide spreads with the current, huge numbers of small 'worthless' fishes and invertebrates are killed. Soon, the reef looks as though it has been hit by a neutron bomb. Once on board, the fish is placed in a tank with fresh water, where it normally revives. Sometimes it dies, but to the mind of the cyanide diver the supply is endless. The larger fishes are held in floating cages, waiting to be picked up by specially designed boats from Taiwan and Hong Kong. Cyanide fishing targets fishes, such as ribbon eels, that are highly prized in the aquarium trade and larger species, such as napoleons or groupers, which are a delicacy in Chinese restaurants, where customers select them from a tank. The deadly cyanide does not harm humans because it is stored in the liver and not in the flesh of the fish.

Diversity: The diversity of an ecosystem can be quantified by the number of species present, otherwise known as the species richness.

However, scientists commonly calculate a diversity index, which takes into account not only the species richness, but also the relative abundance of each species and how closely the species are related. Consider this simplified example about two areas. One has ten different species of wrasse, all from the same genus. The other has eight species from different taxonomic groups, e.g. a scorpionfish, a ray, a turtle, a shrimp, a sea star, a coral, an octopus and a nudibranch. Which area is more diverse? The first area has a higher species richness, whereas the second has a higher diversity index. Coral reefs are considered diverse ecosystems, because in addition to the high number of species they support, the species come from a wide range of taxonomic groups and this abundance is not dominated by a few species.

Fish: This term is used when referring to one or several individuals of the *same* species. For example, 'I saw several mandarin fish on one dive,' i.e. many individuals of the same species.

Fishes: This is a plural form used when referring to two or more individuals of *different* species. For example, 'I saw several frogfishes on that dive,' i.e. many different species.

Gr: Word of Greek origin.

Hermatypic coral nutrition: Corals receive nutrients from several sources, whose relative importance continues to perplex scientists. Nutrition is primarily derived from the organic compounds produced via photosynthesis from their internal symbiotic algae (zooxanthellae). Specifically, the coral polyp uses 94-98% of all organic carbon produced by zooxanthellae. The process of photosynthesis enables hermatypic corals to deposit their limestone skeletons two to three times faster in the light than in the dark. By accelerating the calcification rate, photosynthesis enables reefs to grow faster than the erosion caused by the sea or marine organisms. Hermatypic corals supplement their diet by capturing plankton with their polyps. In addition, corals consume excess zooxanthellae and are able to absorb dissolved organic compounds and bacterio-plankton from the water. Sorokin (see References, p. 254) determined the average nutritional inputs for a range of corals on the Great Barrier Reef as follows: photosymbiosis 70%, feeding on plankton 20% and absorption of dissolved organic matter 10%. Other scientists mention that photosymbiosis covers up to 98% of the coral's total food requirements. These numbers are variable and depend on several factors, including of course the species of hermatypic coral studied. Photosymbiosis dominates, but predation of plankton and the absorption of dissolved organics from the water are also important in hermatypic coral nutrition. The relative importance of these processes depends also on external factors, such as the light levels, which are determined by depth. Plankton predation becomes more important when the coral is deeper and, as a result, less light is available for photosynthesis. It is interesting to note that a coral occupies several levels of the food web at one time. It acts as a primary producer, a herbivore and a carnivore.

Hermatypic symbiont corals: These corals are characterised by symbiotic algae (zooxanthellae) in the cells of their polyps. Their nutrition and growth depends to a great extent on algal photosynthesis and, as a result, they are restricted to shallow sunlit tropical waters. They are the reef-building hard corals that are responsible for constructing coral reef empires. These massive structures result from the accumulation and cementation of hard coral skeletons over thousands of years. Note that there are also some ahermatypic corals that contain zooxanthellae, but do not produce calcareous skeletons, and therefore are not involved in reef building.

House reef: The coral reef in front of a diving resort.

Invertebrate: Animal with no backbone. Most members of the animal kingdom are invertebrates. This incredibly successful group represents 98% of all animal life.

KBR: Kungkungan Bay Resort.

L: Word of Latin origin.

Muck dive site: An area that is characterised by mud, sand and debris, without any of the colourful features encountered on a typical coral reef. Such a site may appear barren, but in fact houses fascinating diurnal and nocturnal creatures such as seahorses, octopuses, snails, stargazers, frogfishes, scorpionfishes, sea cucumbers, etc.

Octopus regulator: A spare regulator to be used in an emergency, for example, in order to share air with a fellow diver who is out of air.

Pelagics: fishes or marine mammals that live in the open ocean, such as whales, dolphins, various sharks, manta rays, tuna, swordfish, marlin, etc. The word pelagic is derived from the Greek *pelagos*, meaning open ocean.

Phytoplankton: Microscopic plants, mostly algae, that float near the water surface.

Plankton: Microscopic plants (phytoplankton) and animals (zooplankton) found drifting in the water. The word is derived from the Greek *planktos*, meaning to wander or drift.

Primitive: When we say that bubble shells or crinoids have primitive characteristics, this does not mean that they lack complexity. The word is used to denote that their characteristics show the least change from their presumed ancestral condition.

School/Shoal: A group of fish that remains together through social interaction is called a shoal. On nearly every visit to a coral reef, you will see fish aggregated together in shoals which range in size from a few individuals to many hundreds of thousands, and may contain a number of species. A school is as a type of shoal, but has greater cohesion between individuals: it is defined as a group of evenly spaced fish, swimming at about the same speed, in the same direction. Schools typically consist of a single or a few closely related species. (Since both words are in common usage, the definitions are not rigorously adhered to.) The main reason for shoaling is as a refuge from predators. Not only is there safety in numbers, but shoals can act as an active defence mechanism, by confusing predators with innumerable and indistinguishable targets. On the reef, fish such as fusiliers and silversides may be seen using these tactics to escape capture. In general, shoals break up when their members feed, so as to reduce the competition between individuals. However, herbivorous surgeonfishes, parrotfishes and rabbitfishes often form mixed groups to feed on the 'gardens' of algae of territorial damselfishes and surgeonfishes, by overwhelming their defences with numbers. Many coral reef fishes also aggregate to spawn, and these include species of groupers, fusiliers, wrasses, surgeonfishes, parrotfishes, snappers and goatfishes.

Scientific Name: Although it might appear easier to communicate with common names, you would soon find this confusing, since a single species may have a number of different common names depending on the region. The Swedish botanist, Carolus Linnaeus, solved this problem in the mid-18th century by devising a universal standard for naming organisms. The resulting scientific names consist of two parts that are usually of Greek or Latin origin. The first part is the genus or generic name and the second is the species or specific name. Scientific names appear in italics. Let us take the example of *Chromodoris leopardus*. The genus, *Chromodoris*, tells us that we are dealing with a nudibranch that shares similar characteristics with other Chromodorid nudibranchs, i.e. nudibranchs belonging to the family Chromodorididae. The species, *leopardus*, indicates which particular nudibranch we are talking about. When you see *Chromodoris* sp., this means that we are sure only of the genus and that scientists have not yet classified the species. *Chromodoris* cf. *leopardus* means that the genus is Chromodoris and the species possibly *leopardus*; cf. *Chromodoris leopardus* indicates that we are unsure of both the genus and the species. *Chromodoris* spp. means that several Chromodorid species are present in the photo.

Scuba: Self-Contained Underwater Breathing Apparatus.

Subal: An Austrian manufacturer of underwater housings for various Nikon cameras.

Ultralight Control Systems: An American supplier of modular strobe arms and camera trays for various underwater cameras and housings.

Wall: A vertical drop-off on the coral reef.

Zooplankton: Microscopic animals that swim in the water column and drift with the currents. Many of the inhabitants of the coral reef have larval stages that disperse in the zooplankton community.

Zooxanthellae: Minute unicellular algae organisms, which live symbiotically within the cells of various marine organisms such as hermatypic corals, tridacnid clams and anemones. They belong to a group of single-celled brown plants called *dinoflagellates*. They require sunlight in order to provide food to their host via photosynthesis. As a result, their host is restricted to sunlit shallow tropical waters.

(10cm): Numbers in parentheses appear next to the species name in the captions, referring not to the size of the particular animal in the photograph but to the maximum size that has been recorded for an adult of that species.

ACKNOWLEDGEMENTS

A book project is a daunting task, particularly when it is one's first. Mark Ecenbarger from Kungkungan Bay Resort gave me the opportunity to fulfil a dream; I thank him for his trust and generous support. Singapore Airlines Greece arranged for the transportation of 150 kilos of equipment; I thank them for allowing me to board the aircraft, despite the fact that I arrived at the Athens airport with baggage weighing 220 kilos. Alkistis Tricha, unfailingly helpful throughout the project, had the privilege of spending hours over the light table sorting over 25,000 slides. She was rescued by Nafsika Athanassoulis, who has been a constant source of encouragement. Argyro Petrinou provided invaluable logistics support.

I am grateful to David W. Behrens, who offered to do the scientific editing of the book and provided valuable assistance throughout the project. Also, to Dr Arthur Anker, Dr Ronald Fricke, Dr Anthony C. Gill, Dr Michael P. Janes, Dr Keiichi Matsuura, Dr Alexander Mustard, Dr Mark Norman, Dr Stuart G. Poss, Dr John E. Randall, Dr David G. Smith and Dr Richard Winterbottom for their scientific advice. Mary Kitroeff edited the first draft and Caroline Taggart polished the final result. George Thompson did an outstanding job with the scanning of my slides. Maro Hadziconstanti combined all the bits and pieces into a wonderful design. Andreas Andreou, Vangelis Chronopoulos, Nikos Kakouris, Antonis Kolias, Antonis Rigopoulos and Vassilis Thymianos played an important role in the production process of the book. Hopefully, they are all still friends.

Steve Warren was the first person who expressed his appreciation for my potential in underwater photography. I thank him for his genuine friendship. The pioneer British underwater photographer, Colin Doeg, consistently succeeded in restraining my Mediterranean temperament with his good sense. I was fortunate to start this adventure 'accompanied' by such friends. In Indonesia, I made many more. Captain Billy Matindas impressed me with his vision and efforts to preserve the Lembeh Strait. Alex Rorimpandey and his family made me feel at home with their generous hospitality. Haslinda Tukunang, Rustam Talengkera, Maurits Rompah, Norma Sinaga and Lidia Kirojan solved all my practical day-to-day problems with a smile. Without the constant medical assistance of doctor Hans Gunawan, I would have been unable to complete the project due to severe sinus problems.

The Kungkungan Bay Resort Dive Team has been crucial in the making of this book. Therefore, if you do not like the book, they are partly to blame… But, jokes aside, there are no words that can adequately express my gratitude for their assistance and friendship. They helped locate many of the subjects and advised me how to view their underwater wonderland. At the same time, they made sure that I survived to tell the story. These were my guardian angels, in alphabetical order: Semuel Bukasiang, Robin Burungmanis, Darkus Daluwu, Dante Gumolung, Paulus Kaangkung, Nuswanto Lobbu, Abner Mangole, Jandry Maninggolang, Iwan Muhani, Ronald Sarante, Derdy Senduk, Wilson Serang, Liberty Tukunang, Ali Umasangadji and Hengki Ungkey.

The Ocean Optics Team in London and Vassilis and John Geramas in Athens were in the unenviable position of trying to satisfy my photographic needs and supporting me while in the field. Many thanks also to Gray Levett from Grays of Westminster, Terry Schuller and Dave Reid from Ultralight Control Systems, Herb Raphael from Sunset Photo Centre and Peter Rowlands.

Opposite: Nudibranch, Chromodoris fidelis (4cm), on scorpionfish.

Fred Bavendam generously offered his expertise, great teamwork underwater, technical advice and companionship. Max Gibbs, Zafer Kizilkaya and Takamasa 'Tono' Tonozuka shared numerous dives. Tono did everything in his power to assist me in a serious camera flood. John Williams shared long and spectacular night dives; Anna and Manfred Wakolbinger were great dive buddies, despite the fact that I envied Manfred his Subal F5 camera housing; and the Haldi family became marvellous friends. Kathi Lomba and Miki Tonozuka were among the many KBR guests who spotted unusual animals and assisted me in my photography. With Roger Steene, we shared luxurious KBR breakfasts and enjoyable chats. Roger's opinions and encouragement served as a benchmark, since he saw the 'first cut'.

Cathy Church opened my eyes to the underwater world years ago. Apart from teaching me underwater photography, Cathy set the foundations for the way I perceive the marine environment today.

The contribution of the people I have mentioned was invaluable, but there were others who generously offered their help and encouragement. Manos & Mariki Anagnostou, Maria Anthouli, Panagis Athanasoulis, Giannis Axabanopoulos, Jeremy Barnes, Alexander Batsas, Andrew Bell, Yuliana Betah, Harry Bougadellis, Grant Bradford, Terry Bradford, Athanasios Chronopoulos, Ed Colijn, Matthew Crowther, Alekos Deligiannis, George Diamantopoulos, Takis Dimitriadis, Takis Dimitriou, Kathryn Ecenbarger, James Er, Greg Gapp, Colin Godsave, Anestis Haidopoulos, Jari Heikkinen, John Hollingshead, Lodewik Kadamehang, Alki Kakaki, Maria Kakouri, Mariano Kaparang, Maria Kapineki, Susan Kehagia, Antonis Kolias, Nikos Koutsopanos, Laurence Lau SeeWong, Ridwan Londa, Syaban Mamonto, Harry Margaritis, Yunus Masala, Ray McNeir, Anestis Nikitaras, Helen Pain, Manuela Palligini, Eugenia & Christina Petrinou, Christos Pozidis, Silvester Benny Pratasik, Andrew Pugsley, Harry Ricketts, Ninny Ruata, Nikos Seitis, Elina Simigdala, Dimitris Skourogiannis, Larry Smith, Merlin Taguriri, Sidharth Thaker, Claire Thompson, Dr Toss, Labis Triantafilopoulos, Nafsika Tricha, Antonia Trichopoulou, Zaira Tseliou, Giota Tsikontouri, George Tsinidis, Atrianjte Ungke, Panagiotis Varsos, Thodoris Varvaras, Sofia Vougidou, Janice Williams, Dimitrios Zagas, Vasilios Zagas, George Zontos. I would also like to thank all those Kungkungan Bay Resort guests who shared their subjects with me, offered their assistance, waited patiently on board until I ascended from my long dives and saved me some fruit. Last but not least, I must note that Kungkungan Bay Resort has approximately 100 employees. I wish to thank them all for their friendliness and good humour.

Afterword: When I arrived in North Sulawesi, I had serious sinus problems that caused excruciating pain during my ascents and descents. I simply could not dive and the whole project was at risk. I was able to complete my 320 dives only by taking very powerful steroids. Although my doctor, Hans Gunawan, warned me about the long-term health risks involved, I felt that I could not abandon the project. Professionals sometimes need to take risks that vacationing divers simply would not consider. Upon completing the book, it was apparent that I was going to have either to solve my sinus problems or to stop diving. I felt as though my whole life was about to collapse. Fortunately, thanks to the expert consultation by doctor John King and the surgical dexterity of doctor Dennis Mendonça, I am back where I belong: underwater. There are no words to express my gratitude for these individuals. To me they are simply *Olympians*.

This page: Members of the KBR dive team in contrasting moods. Ali Teman Umasangadji (top), Nuswanto Lobbu, Iwan Muhani and Wilson Serang.

Opposite: Crab, cf. Porcellanella sp., on soft coral.

Page 252: Nudibranch, Fryeria menindie (5.4cm).

Page 255: Radial filefish, Acreichthys radiatus (7cm).

REFERENCES

Abbot, R. T. & S. P. Dance. 1998. *Compendium of Seashells: A full-color guide to more than 4,200 of the world's marine shells.* Odyssey Publishing: El Cajon, California, USA.

Allen, G. 1996. *Marine Life of Malaysia and Southeast Asia.* Periplus Editions: Singapore.

Allen, G. 1997. *Marine Fishes of Tropical Australia and South-East Asia.* Western Australian Museum: Perth, Western Australia.

Allen, G. R. 1991. *Damselfishes of the World.* Mergus Publishers. Melle, Germany.

Allen, G. R. & R. Steene. 1994. *Indo-Pacific Coral Reef Field Guide.* Tropical Reef Research: Singapore.

Allen, G. R., R. Steene & M. Allen. 1998. *A Guide to Angelfishes & Butterflyfishes.* Odyssey Publishing/Tropical Reef Research.

Anderson, C. 2000. *An Underwater Guide to Indonesia.* University of Hawaii Press: Honolulu, Hawaii.

Anwar, R. 1975. *Kisah-kisah Zaman Revolusi (Stories from the Revolution Era).* Pustaka Jaya: Jakarta, Indonesia.

Archer, J. 1988. *The Behavioural Biology of Aggression.* Cambridge University Press: Cambridge, UK.

Aw, M. 1994. *Tropical Reef Fishes. A Marine Awareness Guide.* Ocean Geographic Media: Pennant Hills, New South Wales, Australia.

Aw, M. 1997. *Tropical Reef Life. A Marine Awareness Guide.* Ocean Environment: Carlingford, New South Wales, Australia.

Bavendam, F. 1999. 'Kungkungan Frogfish Fever.' *Sportdiving,* 73:28-33.

Behr, E. 1990. *Indonesia: A Voyage Through the Archipelago,* Archipelago Press: Singapore.

Bone Q., N. B. Marshall & J. H. S. Blaxter. 1999. *Biology of Fishes.* Stanley Thornes Publishers: Cheltenham, Glos, UK.

Botero, G. & M. G. Pajaro. 1997. 'A future with Seahorses'. *Asian Diver,* 6(1):38-42.

Brown, F. A., Jr. 1940. 'The crustacean sinus gland and chromatophore activation'. *Physiol. Zool.* 13:343.

Bruce, A. J. 1994. *A Synopsis of the Indo-West Pacific Genera of the Pontoniinae (Crustacea: Decapoda: Palaemonidae).* Koeltz Scientific Books: Illinois, USA.

Buckles, G. 1995. *The Dive Sites of Indonesia. Comprehensive coverage of diving and snorkelling.* New Holland Publishers: London, UK.

Coleman, N. 1989. *Nudibranchs of the South Pacific.* Neville Coleman's Sea Australia Resource Centre: Springwood, Queensland, Australia.

Coleman, N. 1994. *Sea Stars of Australasia and their Relatives.* Neville Coleman's Underwater Geographic: Springwood, Queensland, Australia.

Coleman, N. 1998. *Discover Loloata Island. Marine Life Guide to Papua New Guinea.* Neville Coleman's Underwater Geographic: Springwood, Queensland, Australia.

Coleman, N. 2000. *Marine Life of the Maldives.* Atoll Editions: Victoria, Australia.

Colin, P. & C. Arneson. 1995. *Tropical Pacific Invertebrates. A Field Guide to the Marine Invertebrates Occurring on Tropical Pacific Coral Reefs, Seagrass Beds and Mangroves.* Coral Reef Press: Beverly Hills, California, USA.

Cunningham, P. & P. Goetz. 1996. *Pisces Guide to Venomous & Toxic Marine Life of the World.* Pisces Books: Houston, Texas, USA.

Daws, G. & M. Fujita. 1999. *Archipelago. The Islands of Indonesia.* University of California Press: Berkeley, California, USA.

Debelius, H. 1993. *Indian Ocean Tropical Fish Guide.* Ikan Unterwasserarchiv, Frankfurt, Germany.

Debelius, H. 1996. *Nudibranchs and Sea Snails.* Indo-Pacific Field Guide. Ikan Unterwasserarchiv, Frankfurt, Germany.

Debelius, H. 1999. *Indian Ocean Reef Guide.* Ikan Unterwasserarchiv, Frankfurt, Germany.

Debelius, H. 1999. *Crustacea. Guide of the World Shrimps, Crabs, Lobsters, Mantis Shrimps, Amphipods.* Ikan Unterwasserarchiv, Frankfurt, Germany.

Debelius H. & H. A. Baensch. 1997. *Baensch Marine Atlas, Volume 1: The joint aquarium care of invertebrates and tropical marine fishes.* Microcosm: Shelburne, Vermont, USA.

DeLoach, N., A. DeLoach & P. Humann. 1998. 'Isopods: Are they as bad as they look?' *Ocean Realm.* Winter 1998-99:38-39.

DeLoach, N. & P. Humann. 1999. *Reef Fish Behavior: Florida, Caribbean, Bahamas.* New World Publications: Jacksonville, Florida, USA.

Earle, S. E. 1995. *Sea Change: A Message of the Oceans.* G.P. Putnam's Sons: New York, USA.

Edmonds, C. 1995. *Dangerous Marine Creatures. Field guide for medical treatment.* Best Publishing Company: Flagstaff, Arizona, USA.

Erhardt, H. & H. Moosleitner. 1998. *Baensch Marine Atlas, Volume 2: Invertebrates.* Microcosm: Shelburne, Vermont, USA.

Erhardt, H. & H. Moosleitner. 1998. *Baensch Marine Atlas, Volume 3: Invertebrates.* Microcosm: Shelburne, Vermont, USA.

Fautin, D. C. & G. R. Allen. 1997. *Anemone Fishes and their Host Sea Anemones.* Western Australian Museum: Perth, Western Australia.

Fingerman, M. 1969. 'Cellular aspects of the control of physiological color changes in crustaceans.' *American Zoologist,* 9:443.

Fishelson, L. 1990. 'Rhinomuraena spp. (Pisces: Muraenidae): The first vertebrate genus with post-anally situated urogenital organs.' *Marine biology* 105(2): 253-257.

Flannery, T. 1995. *Mammals of the South-West Pacific & Moluccan Islands.* Reed Books: Australia.

Gabbi, G. 1999. *Shells. A guide to the jewels of the sea.* Swan Hill Press: Shrewsbury, UK.

Gaski, A. 1993. *Bluefin Tuna–An Examination of the International Trade with an Emphasis on the Japanese Market.* TRAFFIC International: Cambridge, UK.

Gaski, A. L. & K. A. Johnson. 1994. *Prescription for Extinction: Endangered Species & Patented Oriental Medicines in Trade.* TRAFFIC USA.

Godin, J. J. (editor). 1997. *Behavioural Ecology of Teleost Fishes.* Oxford University Press: Oxford, UK.

Godrej, D. 2001. The No-Nonsense Guide to Climate Change. New Internationalist Publications: Oxford, UK.

Gosliner, T. M. 1987. *Nudibranchs of Southern Africa: A Guide to Opisthobranch Molluscs of Southern Africa.* Sea Challengers: Monterey, California, USA.

Gosliner, T. M. & D. W. Behrens. 1990. 'Special Resemblance, Aposematic Coloration and Mimicry in Opisthobranch Gastropods.' In: M. Wicksten (ed.). *Adaptive Coloration in Invertebrates: Proceedings of a Symposium sponsored by the American Society of Zoologists.* Galveston, Texas, Sea Grant College Program, Texas A & M University.

Gosliner, T. M., D. W. Behrens & G. C. Williams. 1996. *Coral Reef Animals of the Indo-Pacific. Animal Life from Africa to Hawaii Exclusive of the Vertebrates.* Sea Challengers: Monterey, California, USA.

Gosliner, T. M. & D. W. Behrens. 1998. 'Five new species of *Chromodoris* (Mollusca: Nudibranchia: Chromodorididae) from the tropical Indo-Pacific Ocean.' *Proceedings of the California Academy of Sciences.* 50(5):139-165.

Halstead, B. W. 1995. *Dangerous Marine Animals that bite, sting, shock, or are non-edible.* Cornell Maritime Press: Centreville, Maryland, USA.

Halstead, B. 2000. *Coral Sea Reef Guide.* Sea Challengers: Danville, California, USA.

Hanlon, R.T. & J. B. Messenger. 1996. *Cephalopod Behaviour.* Cambridge University Press: Cambridge, UK.

Helfman, G. S., B. B. Collette & D E. Facey. 1999. *The Diversity of Fishes.* Blackwell Science.

Hendler, G., J. E. Miller, D. L. Pawson & P. M. Kier. 1995. *Sea Stars, Sea Urchins, and Allies. Echinoderms of Florida and the Caribbean.* Smithsonian Institution Press: Washington, USA.

Hill, L. 1997. *Shells: Treasures of the Sea.* Könemann: Köln, Germany.

Hoese, D. F. & R. Steene. 1978. '*Amblyeleotris randalli,* a new species of gobiid fish living in association with alphaeid shrimps.' *Rec. Western*

Australian Museum, 6(4):379-389.

Kementrian Penerangan Indonesia (ministry of information). 1954.

Lukisan Revolusi 1945-1950: *Dari Negara Kesatuan ke Negara Kesatuan (Picture of Revolution 1945-1950: From united country to united country)*. Kementrian Penerangan Indonesia: Jakarta, Indonesia.

Kobayashi, Y. 1994. *Micronesian Sea Fishes*. Tokai University Press: Tokyo, Japan.

Kuiter, R. H. 1992. *Tropical Reef Fishes of the Western Pacific Indonesia and Adjacent Waters*. Penerbit P. T. Gramedia Pustaka Utama: Jakarta, Indonesia.

Kuiter, R. H. 1997. *Guide to Sea Fishes of Australia*. New Holland Publishers: Australia.

Kuiter, R. H. 1998. *Photo Guide to Fishes of the Maldives*. Atoll Editions: Apollo Bay, Victoria, Australia.

Kuiter, R. H. & H. Debelius. 1998. *Southeast Asia Tropical Fish Guide*. Ikan Unterwasserarchiv, Frankfurt, Germany.

Kuiter, R.H. 2000. *Seahorses, Pipefishes and their relatives. A Comprehensive Guide to Sygnathiformes*. TMC Publishing: Chorleywood, UK.

Lagler K. F., J. E. Bardach, R. R. Miller & D. R M. Passino. 1977. *Ichthyology*. John Wiley & Sons: New York, USA.

Lieske, E. & R. Myers. 1994. *Collins Pocket Guide – Coral Reef Fishes, Indo-Pacific and Caribbean*. HarperCollins Publishers: London, UK.

Lourie, S. A., A. C. J. Vincent & H. J. Hall. 1999. *Seahorses: An Identification Guide to the World's Species and their Conservation*. Project Seahorse: London, UK.

Marshall, J. G. & R. C. Willan. 1999. *Nudibranchs of Heron Island, Great Barrier Reef. A Survey of the Opisthobranchia (Sea Slugs) of Heron and Wistari Reefs*. Backhuys Publishers: Leiden, Netherlands.

Masuda, H. 1996. *Marine Invertebrates*. Tokai University Press: Tokyo, Japan.

Masuda, H. 1998. *Sea Fishes*. Tokai University Press: Tokyo, Japan.

Masuda, H. 1999. *Guide Book to Marine Life*. Tokai University Press: Tokyo, Japan.

Masuda, H. & Y. Kobayashi. 1994. *Grand Atlas of Fish Life Modes. Color Variation in Japanese Fish*. Tokai University Press: Tokyo, Japan.

Messenger, J. B. 1977. 'Evidence that *Octopus* is colour blind.' *Journal of Experimental Biology*, 70:49-55.

Messenger, J. B., A. P. Wilson & A. Hedge. 1973. 'Some evidence for colour-blindness in *Octopus*.' *Journal of Experimental Biology*, 59:77-94.

Michael, S.W. 1998. *Reef Fishes. A Guide to Their Identification, Behavior, and Captive Care, Volume 1*. Microcosm: Shelburne, Vermont, USA.

Ming, C. L. & P. M. Alino. 1992. *An Underwater Guide to the South China Sea*. Times Editions: Singapore.

Mojetta, A. 1995. *The Barrier Reefs. A Guide to the World of Corals*. Swan Hill Press: Shrewsbury, UK.

Morton B. 1988. *Partnerships in the Sea: Hong Kong's Marine Symbioses*. Hong Kong University Press: Hong Kong.

Moyle, P. B. & J. J. Cech, Jr. 2000. *Fishes: An Introduction to Ichthyology*. Prentice Hall: Upper Saddle River, New Jersey, USA.

Muller, K. 1995. *Underwater Indonesia: A Guide to the World's Greatest Diving*. Periplus Editions: Singapore.

Muller, K. 1995. *Sulawesi – Island Crossroads of Indonesia*. Passport Books: Lincolnwood, Illinois, USA.

Myers, R. F. 1999. *Micronesian Reef Fishes*. Coral Graphics: Guam.

Norman, M. & A. Reid. 2000. *A Guide to Squid, Cuttlefish and Octopuses of Australasia*. University of Melbourne, Australia.

Ono, A. 1999. *Opisthobranchs of Kerama Islands*. TBS-Britannica Co: Tokyo, Japan.

Pechenik, J. A. 1996. *Biology of the Invertebrates*. WCB/McGraw-Hill: Boston, Massachusetts, USA.

Pernetta, J. 1995. *Philip's Atlas of the Oceans*. Reed International Books: London, UK.

Pietsch, T. W. & D. B. Grobecker. 1987. *Frogfishes of the World. Systematics, Zoogeography, and Behavioral Ecology*. Stanford University Press: Stanford, California, USA.

Randall, J. E. 1992. *Diver's Guide to Fishes of Maldives*. Immel Publishing: London, UK.

Randall, J.E. 1995. *Coastal Fishes of Oman*. University of Hawaii Press: Honolulu, Hawaii.

Randall, J. E., G. R. Allen & R. C. Steene. 1997. *Fishes of the Great Barrier Reef and Coral Sea*. University of Hawaii Press: Honolulu, Hawaii.

Ryan, P. 1994. *The Snorkeller's Guide to the Coral Reef, from the Red Sea to the Pacific Ocean*. Crawford House Press: Bathurst, Australia.

Sant, G. 1995. *Marine Invertebrates of the South Pacific – An Examination of the Trade*. TRAFFIC International: Cambridge, UK.

Schram, F. R. 1986. *Crustacea*. Oxford University Press: New York, USA.

Severns, M. & P. Fiene-Severns. 1994. *Sulawesi Seas. Indonesia's Magnificent Underwater Realm*. Periplus Editions: Singapore.

Sorokin, Y. I. 1984. 'The role of heterotrophic non-symbiotic feeding in the energy budget of the common coral species of the Great Barrier Reef of Australia.' *Zhurnal Obshchei Biologii*, 45(6):813-828.

Sorokin, Y. I. 1993. *Coral Reef Ecology*. Springer: Berlin, Germany.

Steene, R. 1990. *Coral Reefs: Nature's Richest Realm*. Charles Letts & Co: London, UK.

Steene, R. 1998. *Coral Seas*. New Holland Publishers: London, UK.

Stone, D. 1997. *Biodiversity of Indonesia*: Tanah Air. Archipelago Press: Singapore.

Sprung, J. 1999. *Corals: A Quick Reference Guide*. Ricordea Publishing: Miami, Florida, USA.

Toer, P. A. 1999. *Kronik Revolusi Indonesia: Jilid II, 1946 (Chronicles of Indonesian Revolution: Part II, 1946)*. Kepustakaan Populer Gramedia: Jakarta, Indonesia.

Tomascik, T., A. J. Mah, A. Nontji & M. K. Moosa. 1997. *The Ecology of the Indonesian Seas, Part Two (The Ecology of Indonesia Series, Volume VIII)*. Periplus Editions: Singapore.

Tudge, C. C. 1995. *Hermit Crabs of the Great Barrier Reef and Coastal Queensland*. University of Queensland: Brisbane, Australia.

Turner, P., B. Delahunty, P. Greenway, J. Lyon, C. Taylor & D. Willett. 1997. *Indonesia*. Lonely Planet Publications: Hawthorn, Victoria, Australia.

Vermeij, G. J. 1995. *A Natural History of Shells*. Princeton Science Library: Princeton, New Jersey, USA.

Veron, J. E. N. 1993. *Corals of Australia and the Indo-Pacific*. University of Hawaii.

Vincent, A. C. J. 1994. 'The Improbable Seahorse.' *National Geographic*, 186:126-140.

Vincent, A. C. J. 1996. *The International Trade in Seahorses*. TRAFFIC International, Cambridge, UK.

Wells, F. & C. Bryce. 1993. *Sea Slugs of Western Australia. A guide to species from the Indian to South-Pacific oceans*. Western Australian Museum: Perth, Western Australia.

Wells, M. J. 1978. *Octopus: Physiology and Behaviour of an Advanced Invertebrate*. Chapman and Hall: London, UK.

Whitten, A. J. & Whitten J. 1992. *Wild Indonesia*. New Holland: London, UK.

Willan, R. C. & N. Coleman. 1984. *Nudibranchs of Australasia*. Australian Marine Photographic Index: Sydney, Australia.

Wilson, R. & J. Q. Wilson. 1992. *Pisces Guide to Watching Fishes. Understanding Coral Reef Fish Behavior*. Pisces Books: Houston, Texas, USA.

Wodinsky, J. 1969. 'Penetration of the shell and feeding on gastropods by Octopus.' *American Zoologist*, 9:997-1010.

INDEX TO PHOTOGRAPHS

Ablabys taenianotus, 26, 224
Acanthaster planci, 218
Acreichthys radiatus, 255
Aeoliscus strigatus, 244
Allogalathea elegans, 69, 155
Alpheus bellulus, 108
Amblyeleotris randalli, 216
Amblyeleotris wheeleri, 216
Amphiprion clarkii, 99
Amphiprion ocellaris, 142
Amphiprion perideraion, 95
Amphiprion polymnus, 109, 140, 141
Amplexidiscus fenestrafer, 96
Antennarius coccineus, 199
Antennarius commerson, 194, 206, 209
Antennarius maculatus, 198, 208, 210
Antennarius nummifer, 207
Antennarius pictus, 30, 106, 107, 145,
        198, 201
Antennarius spp., 111, 212
Antennarius striatus, 196, 197
Apterichthus klazingai, 105
Ardeola speciosa, 24
Arothron mappa, 233
Asthenosoma varium, 82, 83
Astropyga radiata, 2, 88, 90, 91, 192
Balistoides viridescens, 50, 51
Bohadschia argus, 93
Brachypterois serrulata, 225
Calloplesiops altivelis, 222
Canthigaster compressa, 212
Canthigaster valentini, 223
Casmaria erinaceus, 144
Ceratosoma trilobatum, 164, 179
Charybdis spp., 49, 139
Choriaster granulatus, 115
Chromodoris fidelis, 248
Chromodoris geometrica, 169
Chromodoris kuniei, 172
Chromodoris leopardus, 162
Chromodoris strigata, 234
Colochirus robustus, 94
Cryptodromia sp., 74
Cryptopodia sp., 86
Culcita sp., 96
Cyclocoeloma tuberculata, 75, 77
Cymbiola sp., 171
Cypraea sp., 55
Dactyloptena orientalis, 46, 47
Dardanus megistos, 78
Dendrochirus zebra, 4, 29, 225, 230
Dendronephthya, 66
Diadema savignyi, 110
Diodon holocanthus, 104
Discosoma sp., 75, 77
Discotrema sp., 154
Doripppe frascone, 90
Doryrhamphus janssi, 180
Dromia dormia, 74
Echidna nebulosa, 115
Ecsenius namiyei, 231
Ecsenius sp., 227
Entacmaea quadricolor, 98, 99
Eupyrmna morsei, 119
Euselenops luniceps, 169

Eviota pellucida, 226
Flabellina exoptata, 168
Fromia monilis, 149
Fryeria menindie, 92, 252
Fungia fungites, 32
Galathea spinosorostris, 100
Glossodoris averni, 166
Glossodoris cruentus, 172
Glossodoris hikuerensis, 176
Gobiodon okinawae, 218
Halgerda batangas, 137, 163
Heteractis magnifica, 95, 142
Hexabranchus sanguineus, 174
Hippocampus bargibanti, 182, 183, 189
Hippocampus histrix, 186, 187
Hippocampus kuda, 31, 184, 185
Hippocampus sp., 188
Holothuria impatiens, 50
Hoplophrys oatesii, 66
Hydatina physis, 173
Hypselodoris iacula, 179
Hypselodoris maritania, 144
Hypselodoris sp., 176, 179
Inimicus didactylus 49, 202, 203
Junceella sp., 60
Lactoria cornuta, 237
Laticauda colubrina, 44
Lauridromia dehaani, 79
Lauriea siagiani, 71
Linckia laevigata, 113
Lissocarcinus laevis, 101
Lissocarcinus orbicularis, 92, 93
Lutjanus sebae, 192
Lysiosquillina sp., 85
Lysiosquilloides sp., 58
Melibe fimbriata, 158
Metasepia pfefferi, 123
Minous trachycephalus, 215
Muricella paraplectana, 188
Muricella plectana, 182, 183, 188, 189
Naticarius orientalis, 165
Nembrotha purpureolineata, 136, 146
Nembrotha rutilans, 58
Neopetrolisthes maculata, 97
Octopus cyanea, 118, 120, 124, 134
Octopus marginatus, 106, 117
Octopus sp. (mimic octopus), 127-133
Octopus sp. (wonderpus), 53, 125
Octopus vulgaris, 122
Odontodactylus latirostris, 65
Odontodactylus scyallarus, 61, 62
Opistognathus sp., 232
Oratosquilla oratoria, 61
Ovula ovum, 170
Paracentropogon longispinis, 215
Paraluteres prionurus, 223
Paraploactis obbesi, 204
Parascorpaena mossambica, 205
Periclimenes amboinensis, 34
Periclimenes colemani, 54, 83
Periclimenes commensalis, 35, 37, 150,
        157
Periclimenes cornutus, 156, 247
Periclimenes holthuisi, 98
Periclimenes imperator, 93, 114

Periclimenes soror, 112
Periclimenes spp., 87, 96
Philinopsis cyanea, 162
Phyllidia ocellata, 172
Phyllidia sp., 36
Phyllidia varicosa, 242
Phyllodesmium longicirra, 167
Platax teira, 126
Plerogyra sinuosa, 9
Pleuroploca trapezium, 144
Polycarpa aurata, 176, 241, 242
Porcellanella sp., 251
Portunus pelagicus, 110
Pseudanthias squamipinnis, 27
Pseudobalistes flavimarginatus, 52
Pseudoceros bifurcus, 179
Pseudochromis fuscus, 25
Pseudocorynactis sp., 55
Pseudosimnia marginata, 161
Pterocaesio tile, 55
Pteroidichthys amboinensis, 197, 205, 219
Pterois volitans, 7
Reticulidia halgerda, 169
Rhinomuraena quaesita, 148
Rhinopias argolida, 214
Rhinopias frondosa 217
Rhynchocinetes sp., 76
Samaris Cristatus, 72
Scleronephthya sp., 40
Scorpaenopsis sp., 200
Scorpaenopsis venosa, 211
Sepia latimanus, 49, 116, 118, 120, 123,
        138
Sepioteuthis lessoniana, 102, 118
Sicyonia sp., 86
Siderea thyrsoidea , 113
Signigobius biocellatus, 236
Sinularia sp., 42
Siphonogorgia godeffroyi, 223
Solenostomus cyanopterus, 191
Solenostomus paradoxus 183, 190
Stenopus hispidus, 84
Stenopus tenuirostris, 85
Stonogobiops nematodes, 59
Stonogobiops xanthorhinica, 59, 216
Strombus thersites, 162
Synanceia verrucosa, 229
Synchiropus morrisoni, 234
Synchiropus splendidus, 56
Taenianotus triacanthus, 220, 221, 238
Tarsius spectrum, 24
Thecacera picta, 33
Thenus sp., 55
Thysanozoon nigropapillosum, 160
Tozeuma armatum, 39
Tozeuma sp., 86
Trachinocephalus myops, 46, 47
Tridacna gigas, 177
Tubastraea sp., 240
Uranoscopus sulphureus, 228
Vir philippinensis, 9
Xenocarcinus conicus, 45
Xestospongia sp., 76, 199
Zebrasoma scopas, 235
Zebrida adamsii, 91